AND ALL THE LAYERED LIGHT

THE CONECUH SERIES

CELEBRATING DIVERSITY IN THE SOUTH

Like the springs that unite to form the headwaters of the Conecuh River
near Union Springs, Alabama, this series seeks to bring together the
South's many traditions and cultures, celebrating at once our differences
and our commonality.

WADE HALL, SERIES EDITOR

ALSO IN THE CONECUH SERIES

The Outrageous Times of Larry Bruce Mitchell
Waters of Life from Conecuh Ridge: The Clyde May Story
It's Good Weather for Fudge: Conversing with Carson McCullers
Fear Not the Fall: Poems and a Two-Act Drama
Mayor Todd: A Drama

THE CONECUH SERIES

AND ALL THE LAYERED LIGHT

Last Poems

Charles Semones

INTRODUCTION BY WADE HALL

NEWSOUTH BOOKS
Montgomery | Louisville

NewSouth Books
The Conecuh Series
P.O. Box 1588
Montgomery, AL 36102

Library of Congress Cataloging-in-Publication Data

ISBN-13: 978-1-60306-038-7
ISBN-10: 1-60306-038-3

Design by Randall Williams
Printed in the United States of America

TO THE MEMORY OF
MY MOTHER AND FATHER

AND FOR
WILLIAM THOMAS ROYALTY
WITH GRATITUDE FOR ALL THOSE SUMMERS

AND, OF COURSE, FOR
MARLENE
WITH LOVE

CONTENTS

I can't tell if the day is ending, or the world,
or if the secret of secrets is within me again.
—ANNA AKHMATOVA

I know the far-sent message of the years,
I feel the coming glory of the Light
— EDWIN ARLINGTON ROBINSON

The Sabbath Country of Charles Semones

By Wade Hall, Conecuh Series Editor

In late 1962 I moved from Gainesville, Florida, where I was an assistant professor of English at the University of Florida, to Louisville, Kentucky, to join the faculty of a new experimental college named Kentucky Southern. I soon became a member of an informal group of Kentucky poets formed by Joy Bale Boone, who edited a small journal of poetry called *Approaches*. Meetings were usually held either at a poet's home in Louisville or in Elizabethtown; and a young poet from Harrodsburg, Charles Semones, was often present.

I soon learned that he was a talented, driven poet unlike any of the others in the group. He seemed to inhabit another land, another country. Most of his poems were grounded in a place in Central Kentucky he called The Sabbath Country, which I discovered was based on his native Mercer County, and in particular, the rural inhabitants—but not like the ones painted by Thomas Hart Benton or Grant Wood. It is a landscape of sky that Semones has called "a huge despondency of gray"; and below are "subterranean chapels on a shrouded hill," dead elm trees and angels "buzzing like blowflies in a mason jar." There are "ghost-gloomed hollows winding down to bottomland," a screen door that "lets in owl cries," and a poet-lover who strives to be "stoic as a pair of brogans—or a gravestone." It is a Poesque setting where only a beloved's nude body is "a lantern lit against the coming dark." Indeed, the poet and the citizens of his poetic landscape are haunted and obsessed with making connections with God and man that cannot connect and cannot last. He's not exactly a pessimist or an optimist, although he is a poet of extremes. He is, rather, an American latter-day Romantic, passionately pursuing impossible dreams, one after another. Once you enter this real and imaginary world of Charles Semones, you will not forget it. We are delighted to add his *And All the Layered Light* to our Conecuh Series.

In the mid-1970s, Semones accompanied me and another friend, Gregg Swem, to my family home near Union Springs, Alabama. Semones's visit then to the Confederate Cemetery behind Trinity Episcopal Church (now The Red Door Theatre), prompted the poem below, which is a bridge between his native Kentucky and Alabama, where the Conecuh Series originates.

THE CONFEDERATE CEMETERY: UNION SPRINGS, ALABAMA

for Gregg Swem

The long gaze toward eternity begins here
in the weathered eyes of the Confederate soldier
who holds his marble stance
above the decadence of grass and vines
no hands attend.

The tall trim pines keep vigilance
like grim paternal angels.
You observe the rusty wrought iron fence
enclosing those who wished to lie apart.
What was their pride?
And in what particle of dust
is it now reposing?

The flora spreads out like a mother's
or a sweetheart's fan:
the coolness comes but faintly
across suspended years,
through tears that fell where we now move
like some monks uncowled except with wonder.

I sense your mood. This is no place for talk.
We must not interrupt such stillness
with so much as whispers.
This silence, like the fragile stained glass windows
of this boarded-up, abandoned church,
reflects that other century
and the lives that vanished in a cannon's breath.

What loves existed in these perished hearts
we cannot estimate,
and, leaving by an unmarked path,
we cannot relate
to those who shuffle down the little town's
white, glaring streets.

It is a mystery we share by special grace:
Inscrutable as God's averted face.

Acknowledgments

Grateful acknowledgment is made to the editors of the following publications in which some of the poems collected here first appeared, some in different forms:

Ancient Paths: "Bright Canaan" and "Incident in Jerusalem"; *Arts Across Kentucky*: "After Your Leaving on a New Assignment" and "American Autumn"; *Branchwood Journal*: "The Apostle John on Patmos," "At the River," and "The Young Preacher's First Christmas Eve Sermon to the Congregation of the Cowskill River Baptist Church"; *The Kentucky Anthology*: "Christmas Eve"; *The Mennonite*: "Mourning Dove," "Old 100th," "Patmos," "Plain Talk to Hubble, Reading the Bible Backward" and "Walking Through the Bible"; *The South Carolina Review*: "Breakfast at Beaumont Inn on an April Sunday" and "Wildflowers" (formerly entitled "The Widower")

A SPECIAL WORD OF THANKS goes to James H. Miller for his perception, computer skills, and support during a critical time in the preparation of this collection. I hope he knows how much I value his friendship.

THE TITLE OF THIS BOOK is taken from a line of the poem "Bearded Oaks" by Robert Penn Warren.

AND ALL THE LAYERED LIGHT

Breakfast at Beaumont Inn on an April Sunday

Our little town has raised its shades
only enough to gauge the weather.
Last night on the late news there was talk of storms
waking up in the foulest of moods this morning
& proceeding to play havoc with everyone's sleep.
So far there's been only a considerate shower.
It's only nine o'clock
& folks for whom it's not a habit haven't yet
decided whether or not they'll visit God today.
They figure Palm Sunday's alleluias ought
to have been enough to pull them through
to Pentecost & sleeping in this morning seems appealing.
Our deciding to forgo another sermon
this soon after Easter wasn't hard to do. We've kept
in touch with a smattering of e-mails
& a couple or three phone calls, infrequent
as a total eclipse of the sun in this hemisphere.
You flew the better part of yesterday & called
from the inn last night to tell me you'd arrived.
Now, from the parking lot, I see you sitting
on the steps. As I approach, you start toward me,
offsetting a year of absence. We greet each other
under the ginkgo tree in front. In its cloister of branches,
there is delirium; the birds are taking their places
in the choir loft & warming up for worship.
Seated in the dining room, we make small talk
& wait for coffee before going to the buffet

where the end result of Southern culinary art
is amply evident; where the inn is flaunting one of those charms
that keep its well-heeled clientele
returning to an antebellum past time & again.
Sitting here, we're not in the present tense,
not present in a century that hasn't time for
all the goodnesses & graces that flourished here
when that genteel century was in its heyday &
a boozing Stephen Foster might have sat down
at the rosewood grand in the parlor
& flustered hearts with
"Open Thy Lattice, Love"—though it's unlikely
that he ever stayed here. No early register
has a signature to show it.
But more than a hundred years ago,
there were those who loved in upstairs rooms
until loving became a sickness, a wasting away
for want of love *imagined* rather than felt,
there being no question that love ranks high
in the hierarchy of things that hurt.
We speak of a lady, famous once,
all but forgotten now, who lived near here.
She knew the human heart inside out & wrote nervy,
important stories & novels. She's behind
our being together here for breakfast.
We're her devotees. We have that in common.
This is *her* weekend—this last weekend of April every year.
It's the reason for your annual visit. Later, always the scholar,
you'll honor her in forums at the college, just outside
the town she loved & where she's been buried
more than sixty years. Tuesday morning, you'll be
on a flight across the continent again,

outpacing the sun, heading for the coast,
getting back the hours you lost coming to Kentucky.
Given favorable winds, perhaps we'll see each other
when the inn's ginkgo tree quivers
with bird-hymns again next April.

THE REVENANT AT 'HALCYON'

(Elkton, Todd County, Kentucky)
In Memoriam: Joy Bale Boone and George Street Boone

Be mindful of the time and distance it's returning from,
its need to feel a sense of place. Wait as it examines
the front porch columns brought years ago
from Nashville's replica of the Parthenon.
Once inside, imagine its placing antimacassars
on the backs and arms of the two matching wing chairs,
unmoved from where they were, facing each other
in the family room where the walls are lined,
floor to ceiling, with sagging shelves of books,
most of them read. See how it takes its ease
and slouches there—quite unlike itself,
out of character—but bolts upright when, suddenly,
"Für Elise" lilts faintly from the out-of-tune grand piano
in the dated parlor where, some nights,
the same ancestor's portrait falls from its nail
above the mantelpiece,
and will not stay put—it mattering not how many times,
or how carefully, it's hung back in its place.
Now take notice of how lightly it touches
the serving trolley holding the liqueurs and Scotch
in readiness for the evening's drinks. Watch how it slinks,
seductive as a bride, into the wide hall and listens
at the foot of the curving stairway before starting up.
Observe its pausing on each step. Consider what it hears,
or does not hear, beyond the landing. Mark well how,

not discomposed, it takes into account
the second-story rooms—held in the hush of absence,
the subtle thrall of decadence. Study how,
as a bridegroom would, it selects an heirloom bed
suited to the long-awaited night of love.
Then ponder its wandering the lawn,
imagine its admiring peonies and iris in profusion,
the nods of lilac panicles at twilight,
and the fringe tree's fragrance lingering at dusk.
Marvel how it has come back again,
how it intends to live here now for good.
The irrefragable urging of blood's ancestral memory
will not abandon this grand house to the vagaries
of an ungracious century. A ghostly meandering
turns time counterclockwise: anyone entering here
would see that everything has changed,
yet everything's the same. There is an ineffable presence,
a sameness strangely undiminished.
Should you be the one who comes, mind how
in a proud family's plot in the small town's cemetery,
the deft, fulgent moon of April returns
and stitches an intricate tapestry
of antique light to cover a new grave.

Lee and Grant Have Coffee Together at Starbucks after the Surrender at Appomattox

Wait up, General. I'd hoped we could go
into Appomattox for a cup of coffee
when that official folderol was put to rights
for our secretaries to make final copies of.
As I think I told you earlier, I've got the mother
of all migraines, and coffee is about the only thing
that gives me any ease. Besides, I think you and I
ought to talk, somewhere private,
away from all that orchestrated politeness
back there in McLean's parlor. Of course,
I know how it is. You can't end a war as quick and easy
as saying Amen when you get done praying.
There's got to be a big to-do such as we've seen
this afternoon—men shuffling important papers,
getting them ready for us to sign in triplicate.

          Listen! Is that a mockingbird I hear over there
in that clutch of trees in the corner of the yard?
Nice sound, isn't it? Do you think?
Oh, couldn't be . . . Why would the Almighty
tell a bird something so important?
Still, it makes a body wonder.
I see the word's already made it into the village.
I hear the sexton at one of the churches
giving the bell rope all he's got. Apt as not it's the Methodist.
Those folks tend to get the news out as soon

as something happens. But you can bet
the Presbyterians and Episcopalians will wait
and announce it at meeting come next Sunday.
And what's funny is by then everyone
will have heard it anyway.
But that's how they are—never given to excitement.
Now as far as those saintly souls over yonder
at the Baptist church, well, they're apt to throw
one of their protracted meetings, claiming the Lord
should get the credit for what happened.
Now, General, I know you're a religious man—but riddle me
this, will you? How *exactly* did the Lord have a hand
in putting an end to the butchery we've been going at
tooth and nail for the last four years?
Well, I guess it's a matter of *interpretation*,
how one chooses to look at it. So let them
get themselves built up into a frenzy if that
will put the icing on their cake. To each his own
is what I say. That's what I try to live by,
though I fail miserably at times. And when I get it right
I credit it to luck. To change the subject,
isn't this as fine an April as any mortal ever looked upon?
I notice the lilacs are especially forthcoming
this year—the bulging panicles dripping their
white and lavender, fragrancing the air, making it
smell the way that heaven must on its best days.
Makes me think a poet might sit down and
write a poem about the lilacs as sure as I'm hearing
your footfalls on these cobblestones.

        I'd be remiss, General, if I failed to tell you
that your ragtag bunch of men and boys

gave us all we could say grace over—and then some.
I know for a fact that old Lincoln thinks the same way too.
But what you've done was best, sir,
even though I know it took the hide. Of course,
I don't have to tell *you* the odds were stacked
against your pulling off a victory,
that it was a case of two plus two adding up to four,
which any schoolchild knows.

    Here we are.
I'd hoped we'd find it open. General, I see a table
over by the window. We'll take it if that suits you.
I like to look at lilacs. There's nothing that's more pleasing
to the eye on an afternoon like this one.
They are especially lovely to gaze upon here
in your Virginia, just as they are up in Washington.
And, General, has it crossed your mind
that it's Palm Sunday? I feel sure it has. It occurred to me
this morning when I was doing my ablutions.
Now that makes these proceedings almost sacred,
like a piece of scripture or some old hymn
we've always known. When the war was at its worst,
my Julia was always sending me a new one.
I've got a number of them tucked inside my head.
But I can't sing a note. By the way, I hope you feel
that I was fair with you in our settling up,
by letting your men and boys keep their horses and mules.
They'll soon be needing them for putting out their crops.
It's getting to be that time.

    I hope you know
I wish them well, General, and that goes doubly so for you

after all you've been through—the loss of your
right-hand man that you called Stonewall being such a blow,
to name but one calamity, just one of many.
But now, thank God, the spilling of blood is ended
and the wounded land and hearts can start their mending.
You know, I don't think we ever were
as much different as we are alike.
It was the barrel-bellied politicians with their
fancy watches and fobs
that mostly got our particular Armageddon going.
They were jawing war-talk before the first shot was fired
on Sumter. Dirty money changed hands
and palms got greased aplenty like those not
in the know would not believe. *They* think
it was entirely the business about the slaves.
Well, General, I could tell them a thing or two,
and so could you. But I've noticed you're not
big on words, not one to say more than's necessary.
I see you've finished your coffee. If you'd like
we'll head back to where we hitched our mounts.

        I declare, it does look like that fellow's going
to ring the bell the livelong afternoon
till full dusk comes and puts an end to it.
And that mockingbird—it's still at it too.
Isn't it a wonder? But, come to think of it,
looked at another way, it is no wonder. To be honest,
it's not sinking into *me* as easy as I'm letting on.
It'll take some getting used to. But I believe
my migraine's letting up, thanks to some decent coffee
and the certainty of stress slacking off.
Just think—we have delirious birdsong

instead of rifle-clatter on this day
when Christ rode into Jerusalem on a borrowed donkey.
I figure the Almighty's up there smiling.
Wouldn't surprise me if he doesn't have heaven's
congregation playing their banjos and fiddles
and maybe raising a descant over what happened
at half-past two or so this afternoon.
I declare that mockingbird's breast is fixing
to burst wide open. It seems to me that beauty's
made a comeback, no doubt about it.
Perhaps in time—after *our* time,
yours and mine—the Shenandoah will be abloom
with the light of stars death snatched
from the eyes of our doomed boys.

In Redbud Winter, Haven Clary Remembers the Dogs of His Life

It seems that it's always near twilight on an afternoon
in redbud winter when a slur in the wind
says their names as plain as any human voice could.
And they come back, not as transparent ghost-dogs
or dog-ghosts, but as their furry selves,
just as they were back then, and resume their lives
in this place they knew every inch of when they
were alive here once with him. They come back,
looking no different than when they went away but,
as he soon discovers, they are neither visible nor invisible.
He's aware of them only as tactile *presences*.
It's as if they're leaping on him or licking his hand,
for instance. He senses them close on his heels
as he tries to finish his chores before good dark sets in,
and he must light the cast-off lantern, low on oil,
he found rusting. He doesn't live here anymore;
he has not for longer than he can easily remember,
given his unrelenting circumstance.
The place is abandoned to whatever wildness will have it.
He knows *that* because of where he lies now—day in, day out.
Being dead, he sees it more clearly than
when he was alive here. It's only moments
from the Deep Creek churchyard,
lorded over by disputatious crows.
He notices the clapboard house, long uninhabited,
has fallen into ruin. So has the tobacco barn,
a haven for owls and groundhogs. The woodshed

and corn crib are leaning; the cowbarn
where hay-scent and cows' breath mingled
with the fresh milk-smell is without
its roof—and rotting boards, still holding on,
sag outward. Someday a quirky gust will rip them off,
leaving the frame, skeletal and grim, to meaner weathers.
Brownie, Pepper, and Gayheart check out everything in sight.
They were strays that showed up at his back door.
He gave them food and refuge and,
as he hoped they would, they stayed.
But years of redbud winters added up
and made them old and lame. When the time came,
each one limped away to a dying place,
chosen long beforehand. He knew what they were up to;
he knew some instinct not meant for him
to comprehend had told them what to do.
He watched them struggle down the hollow
below the house, behind what was once
his mother's garden, and never made a move
to call them back, though a hot stone weighted down
his heart and, being no stranger to loss,
he got bleary-eyed as they labored out of sight.
It wasn't for a lack of love that he let them go.
He knew they were doing nature's bidding,
and he felt he'd always known that
what comes natural to man or beast is better left alone,
not tampered with in the God-stun of its happening.
Some other redbud winter coaxes them away
from their sun-bleached bones, the wreckage of their skulls.
And they show up again on April days
when redbud-tapers flare in the long hush
of cedar-dusk. Watching his dogs

from where his death has coffined him,
he's mindful all over again of the brevity
of any creature's time on earth.
It was yesterday, it seems, or the day before,
that he was a boy here doing what boys do
when an urgency more startling
than their first glimpse of God tongue-ties them.
His needling manhood went by without a wife.
He had only his dogs—Bruiser and Gringo and Peso—
for company, and they never let him down;
never wandered off into a winter nightfall,
forcing him to go outdoors in the bitter dark and search for
them. They loved him, and it was their nature to be faithful,
unlike some people who'd deserted him
without a second thought, it seemed.
He'd sensed early on that his life was to be
one of solitude, except for them.
That's when he resolved not to portion
out his time in dribs and drabs.
Though a solitary man, he wanted his being
here to count for something.
He almost thought his every word and deed
could be a kind of psalm.
But when he least expected it, his bones foretold
December and the coming of the long siege of cold.
His dogs were never fretful. Their acceptance of final things
amazed and humbled him.
He thought their stoic poise was something
he could learn from—something that would serve him
well through his young manhood, his edgy
middle age and hoary eldering.
But long before he anticipated it, a voice,

as faint and far away as a mourning dove's,
told him it was time to go—they to fields and woods
where chipmunks scampered unafraid and he,
borne by six stout friends, to Deep Creek's grievous hilltop
where stones were weather-crazed.
Now that his dogs can no longer heed his every footfall,
he finds his grave's as good a place as any in which
to spend an April day, watching it sadden
by the moment to its close.
He has a hunch that heaven's nothing
more than the backcountry he lived in alone, and got old in.
He suspects that, instead of ghosts, his dogs are shaggy angels
looking out for him—the only ones he knows,
the only ones he's apt to know.

FOR GRINGO

(1990–2004)

You'd think I would be getting over it by now,
but there are still days when I'll be dawdling around
the house with maybe something of Schumann's
on the stereo, halfway thinking the phone will ring
almost any minute, and it will be the vet. He'll let
me know that Gringo's routine visit went without
a hitch and assure me everything looked good,
and that Gringo's antsy, missing home. I almost
start to get my keys and wallet, or reach in the closet
for my coat. That's when it hits me how on a morning
last November, Gringo's pain changed how things
had been, and his sudden trip to the vet's was not
like all the others. The vet did not call that day,
or the next one. There was no need to. By week's end,
I was notified the crematory had delivered Gringo's
ashes, and I could pick them up at my convenience.
I keep them in a white box with a subtle gloss, beside
a figurine of St. Francis I bought several years ago
in a pricey shop down the coast below St. Augustine.
That was before I heard of a saucy black Chihuahua
that I'd name Gringo, not knowing that of all the dogs
of my life I'd love him best—and not having an inkling
that a day would come when a squarish marble urn
containing all that's left of me would hold him too.

CHARLES SEMONES   33

WALKING WITH PESO IN CARPENTER'S GRAVEYARD

Peso and I, fond of each other's company,
walk among blurred gravestones,
most of them tilted, many of them fallen,
in Jacob Carpenter's half-acre of perpetual repose
for some who could not wait for January's knee-deep snows
to melt, and others looked away when
late April's peonies were bulging.
Others gave it up when blood-mooned August
blistered fields and souls. And there were those who hung on
until late November's gunmetal-weather of crows.
These folks passed over, and have long been "Asleep in Jesus";
they are "Gone But Not Forgotten" into *knowing*,
or not knowing, what it's all about—the well-kept secret one
must make it to the other side, the ivory palaces to know.
Peso scouts in front of me, eager to see what lies ahead,
her tiny nose pointed groundward, her tail going
like a metronome, not missing a beat—a fawn-colored
five-pound Chihuahua whose face would make a grown man
weep, or want to. I have only questions the dead
are not inclined to answer. They're in no mood for
conversation—not today. I try to figure out what
Peso's thinking, what she might be pondering,
presuming, that is, dogs give any thought to eternal verities.
Most sane men would say that they do not.
The sad truth is that they love life so much
and do not know they'll have to give it up. The dead
brook no interruption of their brown study. I picture
them gazing through undulant distances

to where all their summers coalesce into an equinoctial
glow. I set my mind on names, start taking notice of them:
Bottoms, Comingo and Coyle, Dickerson and Fields
and, just inside the gate, along the fence,
the odd ones, the artist-types I've heard, the Skeelses—three
unwed sisters and their unwifed brother—they
who came here from another state, bringing with them
the notion that the soul sleeps until the Judgment Day,
thus earning for themselves the dubious nickname
"*Soulsleepers*." They built a church just down the road
from here where they could preach their take on the gospel
to the few who were curious, though converts were scarce.
Here too, enclosed by wrought iron fences, are the Tylers,
Wickershams and Yankees. They choose to lie apart.
It would seem that even here there are those pesky social
distinctions where one would not expect to find them.
In a weed-infested corner lies one who was a looker and,
they say, a lover. Peso veers off in the direction of his grave.
The folks—and they are few—who still remember him
say that he was only forty-something when he was
blown away for loving the wrong woman. No one ever
speaks her name. Though at the time it was on everyone's
tongue, just as they knew her husband did not
much approve, and used his 12-gauge to make it plain.
He was cleared, of course, by a jury of his peers,
all of whom said *they* would have done the same thing,
only sooner. Finally I see that nothing's to be gained by this
meandering over what some would call God's half-acre that
Jacob Carpenter gave himself and his neighbors in 1837
to bury the dead in. I have a tangle of thoughts
as Peso and I head back to the world of the living.
For a reason unclear, I intuit Peso knows a thing or two

that she's not telling. Not today. Not ever.
And I don't blame her. If I could guess
at what the dying see when the death rattle stops
and they succumb to their last gasp
for breath, I'd hold such knowledge in my heart.
I'd never breathe a word to anyone.

Lilacs and Snakeskin

With her quaint Sunday shoes and prim black dress,
its tidy collar outspread like dove-wings,
and white as the antimacassars in her parlor
that's gotten fusty from over half a dozen decades
of disuse since her one suitor left,

everybody's quirky maiden aunt knows how it's always
been, and can say it much better. I won't presume
to quote her. I've got enough hard truths of my own
without reciting hers.

The scent of old desire, like the last of April's lilacs,
and the staccato-thrum of snakeskins in late summer,
saddens me. September's wind-slurred adagio stagnates
in the heart like water in a ruined well. We lose by our
own hand what we love too much to throw away.

AFTERWARD

I thought I'd rather love what you were
to me all those felicitous evenings
in lilac-weather when you said our
conversations would last a lifetime.

I knew then that it's my nature
to tire easily of people and things
and want only the excitement
of an idea I've never had before.

But now the snarl of out-of-season thunder
raises my anxiety a decibel or two.
I burrow in a featherbed—not surprised that,
more than anything, what I want back again

are those after-supper moments last November
when I listened for your pebble on the pane.

Mourning Dove

It is the boring tag-end of an uneventful morning
in late May. I sit at my kitchen table while, outdoors,
the headstrong spring is rushing pell-mell toward
the summer solstice. My coffee's getting cold
in the souvenir mug I bought at Walden Pond
while I write a directive—"To Whom It May Concern"
—for my obsequies or, rather, the lack of any.
I'm keeping my last rites simple: no costly, time-consuming
folderol—a quick cremation, no memorial service,
the burial of my ashes on our family plot with those
already there, some of whom I've missed. I do not find
it unsettling, but unexplainably soothing, that there are low
snarls of thunder in the west and every now and then
the five faint notes of a mourning dove sounding far-off,
as distant as heaven, but most likely no farther away
than my next-door neighbor's woods.
I've always thought that of the myriad noises any day brings,
the wistful calling of the mourning dove must come
closest to being what a recurrent pleading
from the other side would sound like.
Let's say that someone who's left the earth for good
is homesick and dissatisfied in spite of what the comfy
never-ending is supposed to be. After too much time
not broken into days and nights that he
was used to here, no fields to plow in spring,
no oak trees to nap under on laid-back summer days,
and no Indian summer afternoons halcyon
with gossamer, he'd likely find a way to send a soulful

CHARLES SEMONES   39

utterance down through boundless altitudes so that we—
provided we are fortunate enough to hear it clearly
as a Sabbath bell—would know beyond a doubt
that it was no ordinary voice and those no ordinary words
we were listening to, but all the proof we need
that our last breath-catch is *not* an end to anything,
but a beginning.
The mourning dove makes five ghost-syllables into a plainsong.
However far away one may seem to be when dawn
reruns creation, and when twilight darkening to dusk
bends the knee for evening prayer,
Christ teaches his apostles the beatitudes or prays,
in extremis, in Gethsemane again. I think of *sacraments:*
baptism and Communion—God's giving us his blessing
to draw near him in the purest of all liquids, water,
and feed on the body and the blood made bread and wine.
There are, beyond an impenetrable distance,
a supplicant's dire pleas for mercy—a penitent's
falling on his face for a last chance at grace.

Maynascence at Beaumont Inn

for S. Dixon Dedman, born 21 May 1981

In a town that wears its history on its sleeve,
where ancestral ties are all but tantamount to holiness,
there is an antebellum mansion, not in decline but thriving,
its ginkgo trees resonant again this year
with ordered sounds—adagios at once passionate and
contemplative—of birds flaunted skyward, a music
we slogged through dreary weeks of hard weather to hear
the first notes of. The year of your nativity it was as
if each day in the month of May insisted on being a Sunday.
Spring was insane, it seemed, with a floral profusion—
the lilacs' purple panicles bulging and drooping,
and the peonies by chimneys and in fencerows nodding
to one another, but not to passersby, like a clique of matrons,
well-bred, accustomed to being coddled.
The earth was defying reason, giddy, spinning on the tip
of God's forefinger, pointing to yet another summer solstice.
Had there been errant angels abroad in the land,
they would have called the season right for a nativity.
And so it was when nature could bear its fullness
no longer that you came into earthlight,
your emergence from the comfy warm
of the watery holding pattern you had been in
accomplished as smoothly as the descants of birds—
not those sedate ones in the choir, but the ones
inclined toward a riotous worship of their own devising.
The physician and nurses in attendance

for your arrival looked on and declared that the baby just
delivered showed every sign of being special.
It was apparent, even in your infancy, that you
had the makings of an excellence rarely seen.
A previously unencountered glow encircled you,
not unlike that of finger lamps weary saints
and others of their ilk must hold high when they trudge
up and down the mostly untraveled backstreets of heaven,
no longer accustomed to darkness, searching for someone
who's lost his way even in paradise.
You wore your boyhood like raiment made of wind.
Attaining manhood, you took the road "less traveled by"—
but with counsel and caution. Even as you threaded
the needle of yourself and the in-and-out
of veinal stitches formed the flesh-hued tapestry
you could be proud of, you took nothing for granted,
having learned that God is not without his vagaries,
mercurial, given to moods of daylight and moonshadows
subsuming each other, the sly gestures unleashing
the slithering snakes of a vast intrigue.
You are twenty-five today, having already made good
on a promise, or what was interpreted as one
by those whose hands blessed your birthing—
they who swore they heard a susurrus
and witnessed a flashing of myriad wings, not common
to this world, descending on your soul aborning.
You're everything expected of you and more.
Once knowing you, one cannot simply like you.
That is a maxim the bone-marrow knows. One is given no
sensible option but to *love* you. We are old men here,
no longer endowed with the gift of our former eloquence.
Knowing how subtly mortality creeps,

how suddenly it seizes, we are not ourselves,
but overwhelmed by the beauty of body and spirit
bequeathed to you by blood. We make a psalm
of your name in our mouths. You serve us
an earthy sacrament we have hungered for.
In the sadness of our eldering, we've acquired the plainest
language—a tongue largely monosyllabic—the better
to signify anointment and entreaty. It is what's
most elemental that counts. There is no time
or place for superfluous flourishes. This is when spring's
constellations spend their small change freely.
The polestar we keep watch by never wobbles off-course.
But our leave-taking is imminent. We huddle
and speak our plain truths plainly. You are wanted here
throughout the stretch of the never-ending. Stay.

Elegy at the Summer Solstice

In Memoriam: Phillip Warren Young
April 13, 1969 – June 22, 1987

I consider it no small change, no run-of-the-mill serendipity
that, unmindful of time, strolling among rows of stones on an
afternoon of dense mist and the last leaves letting go when the
errant, meandering breeze of late autumn was a corpse-cry, I
happened on your grave by accident, and was stunned to the
quick by the handsome marble slab, surrounded by ivy, under
which you lie, your too brief past and your promising future
enshrined in the crucial moment of my imagining. You suffer
yourself beneath that slab with its Celtic cross and the carved
litany of your standout accomplishments. No doubt they fixed
you in the typical posture and so you're propped with your hands
crossed, as if such indifference were your casual response to
what happened. But nobody's convinced, no one's saying you've
let God off easy. Not one soul's forgetting the circumstance of
a gentle rain commencing, making the highway slippery just
outside Atlanta on a summer Sunday. No one wanted to believe
what happened. How could it have happened? The weather was
as dry as a jawbone in the embers of hell when you and your
friend left Lexington. What can one say now except that you've
been left with nothing to do since metal writhing on itself in
a savagery of mood gestured its vile intentions to you? It was
then that you were subsumed by the Eternal Present: the tenses
of your life blurred beyond recognition, the syntax mangled
into gibberish, a baffled, mutilated phrase that trailed off into
the lurid scribble of your death. Although I never knew you, I

sit on the wrought iron bench beside your grave, and consider
art and artifice and harrow words that might be usable to make
appropriate homage—it not mattering that we were strangers.
If I know you at all, it is only, and entirely, through your dying.
I have only the abecedarium bequest of words that Webster left
us, a lexicographic legacy tendered by Sandburg and Millay—
and Patchen who, from his watery grave, reminds us, " . . . there
are/ Many beautiful arms around us and the things we know."
Donald Justice, once the celebrant of declining light, now
drowsing in his greatness, may rouse, bestir himself to utterance
and, if prompted, publish sorrow's psalms for your coming
too soon to those tall beatitudes of air where only the eldering
should be. Do you know how many years I've tried to coax our
native tongue to give you proper due—an imago, a boy who
long back became ethereal? It is a dubious mortality that tethers
me, and so I cherish it all the more the closer I get to that instant
when you forfeited breath and heart and pulsebeat near Atlanta.
I've sensed the cashmere-soft embrace of those dark angels you
had no time to drive a bargain with. Nor would they have been
inclined to hear your offer. With what elegance of wings they
would enfold *me*, an eloquence that's become second nature to
you, but one I do not aspire to. I have work to do, and with
what anticipation I approach it. I do not denigrate the hopsack
sturdiness, the slang and jargon of the commonplace, quite
unlike those foreign languages you had mastered— especially the
Swedish, no longer fluent, silenced on your ruined tongue. The
light of your intelligence is dimmed to invisibility in the cloistral
darkness of your grave, but the cold light of it illuminates the
remembrance of those who knew you. The claim could be made
that you're the lucky one though it's most unlikely you'd agree.
But surely you understand: you are safe from the savageries
of time, the sure eventuality of a beautiful physique's gradual

dissolution, and the ironies of any unwelcome fate that might have come near you if you'd lived longer. I can hear you now, your tone angrily insistent: "I would have settled for my chances. Being dead's no fun. There's no future in it." Surely you were one of the choice examples your generation could hand over as a sacrifice to the frayed, impoverished world in need of the gifts of a brilliant mind and the bounteous spirit you had to offer in abundance. I do not say that those who knew you would have claimed you had no flaw. No teenage boy should be a saint. But even though your humanity may have tempted you into uncertainty of purpose or even moral frailty, your intellect asserted itself, your finest thoughts took precedence, and your athlete's body never once mistook its nearness to perfection for invincibility. It was a starpoint of light in your blood that you had no mediocrity to rise above. You started out ahead and reached magnificence undreamed of by your peers. But a devious circumstance you would never have envisioned had other plans for you a little more than a year away—even as you toured Leningrad, played basketball in Stockholm and, later, when that school year ended, toured the Continent with your parents. It was at the time of the summer solstice back in your native land, that you were doomed to face the beckoning of that whitest light or impenetrable blackness beyond all reckoning. From that split-second on a rain-slick highway, the scene where your mortality was canceled, they brought you home to Lexington where the mortuary of choice could barely hold the relatives and friends who came to pay their last respects at your Friday morning service, with the grave splendor of music, the sedate delirium of roses, the eulogy celebrating you—before the thirty-odd miles to Harrodsburg began in early afternoon. The mourners left you to your rest in Spring Hill Cemetery, in your parents' hometown where, in time, the cyclic seasons and variable weathers claimed

you for their own—a boy, barely eighteen, having forgotten
foreign names and places, foreign phrases that were your portion
once, when the hot vitality of life coursed through you like a
splendid fever. The world, as you had known it, went about
its business, unnaming you. I go there often to honor you, a
youth unknown to me but a kinsman of my spirit, in whose
achievements I find my boyhood's ambitions mirrored, though
never realized as were yours. Now at my age I know the score:
they are the chosen ones who grow holy, whose spirits feed
unceasingly on the animating constancy of God. Perhaps in
some Athenian chamber of the never-ending there are hung for
you tall tapestries stitched with an antique light—resplendent
as the morning star or Atlantis rising from the sea, symbols of
ovations you no longer hear. Tonight the full moon of November
blooms in the cold eastern sky like some exotic flower left over
from a past summer. Its fragrance of light spills amply on your
grave, thought this night will bring the first hard freeze. In that
rectangle of earth where you're spending yourself, having earned
the coinage of eternity, it is possible some cosmic memory
survives and you revisit all those places—Sweden and Russia,
Europe, and the American South where a singular excellence
circled your head like a halo— excellence inviolate still in the
time-defying orient of your death.

*(The passage in quotes is from "The Character of Love Seen as a
Search for the Lost" by Kenneth Patchen.)*

Belated Note to Donald Justice

Famed for syllables of light, though the melancholy light
of summer afternoons, far-flung, subsiding, that glows
softly, softly, and only in remembrance, you left us with
nothing further said about the house in "Southern Gothic"
and whether its decline was so far advanced that, finally,
given ravages of time and aberrations of the weather,
it succumbed, collapsed, became a heap of bricks which
rapacious kudzu seized without delay. You did not say if
it was brick or frame. (I fancied brick—an antebellum
mansion, its once regal columns leaning like old cripples.)
You chose to speak of broken windows and broken eaves
under which not a single nest housed birds and, though
you did not say, one must assume that no birdsong fluted
in the morning, much less at dusk when the homing bee
was dismayed to find no garden where once there'd been
a garden—and surveyed no flowers, nor any evidence of
flowers that had surely bloomed in profusion there. What
haunts one are the roses—wallpaper roses, and no damask
to deter the moon's unraveling. No semblance of a former
elegance remains save for what uncurls, imagining its ruin.

WILDFLOWERS

In Memoriam: Shirley Miller Rowe

A storm is imminent. The leaves are uneasy, heaving their
sibilant glossolalia before the gospel of rain commences
far-off, like a whispery utterance from the never-ending.
Scripture from that beatitude will be bell-toned over her
grave, barely one year old in the sloping churchyard, edging
the backcountry she came from to meet and marry my
friend, bear his son, and stamp her farm woman's style on
every room of the home they didn't share long enough,
before something lacking the kindness of rain seized her,
spoke its feared name, made known its foul intentions
to her body, and foretold the casket spray of wildflowers.
He'd have nothing floristy. Mindful of how she had loved
them—how he loves them now that her garden is his to
tend—he is faithful to her wildflowers. He teaches me their
names: *blue mist, coreopsis, downy skullcap, joe-pye weed,
wild bergamot* . . . These summer afternoons are drone and
screech to one who would have silence with his grief. He
takes wildflowers when he visits her, where the gravestone
has his name on it too. His duck skiff, promising a
diversion, sits in the shed. He's severe with himself. But
come December, he'll put the skiff in the river again and go
duck hunting. The rest of his life will precede his skiff as it's
oared upriver. He'll think how she never minded his being
a hunter. He'll remember her cookery, how she prepared
his kill from her own recipe, and how on wildness they
feasted.

AFTER YOUR LEAVING ON A NEW ASSIGNMENT

In Memoriam: Peter Jennings, 1938-2005

"That is happiness; to be dissolved into something
complete and great." —Willa Cather

No, not incomprehensible. Those Londons,
Cairos, and Beiruts that had been your beat
when you were new to network news
were comprehensible even as they vanished
from your view that Sunday evening in your Manhattan
sickroom, your closest family watchful
at your bedside while yet another country,
one not recognizable, far different from the others
where you'd been commenced assuming an interplay
of light and shadows, a wavery concession
in your sight. It was unlike any previous destination
you had known. In its strangeness, it could have been
Atlantis rising from the sea. You took it to be
the place of your new assignment and perhaps,
for an instant, no more than a split second,
you knew the old anticipation, the instinct for the story
nudging, even in your dying—you the urbane,
consummate professional you'd long back disciplined
yourself to be. The life that you were leaving
had been a good one and you knew it, filled
with the challenges you needed—and allowing
time for love. But you sensed news on the brink
of happening, and your bags were packed,

your passage there secured. You must have intuited
that this would be the big break of your esteemed career,
the story you and others in the field
had thus far been denied access to: whether
there's another side and, if so, what the weather's like,
if its inhabitants are congenial, and if residence
there's to be desired. Oh, not incomprehensible your going—
the essential you dissolving into rock and foam,
that subsumption into something greater
than any world you'd known.

A Boy at Deep Creek Gets the Scoop on God

Once in lilac-weather, the wind-slur, and the little winters of
his fourteenth April, a boy not ordinary, and mostly sad, tried
in excess of what's considered reasonable to fathom matters
everlasting and gave more thought than other boys to God and
what his grand design might be for one who wanted more than
anything earth offered to fit into his scheme. He craved the well-
pleased look of some he thought were saints who, never once
professing to be saints, were saintly nonetheless, even if they'd
never been in exile on the Isle of Patmos, though one would
have thought they had, like the old apostle, John—the one best
loved by Jesus, the sole survivor of the clan. Nor had they read,
or claimed to, the Book of Revelation from the beginning to the
end. They said that, early on, they'd found the pleasures of the
flesh vastly overrated and chucked them for the ways of God
who tramped the sky above the meetinghouse with frightful
footfalls. When August brought the annual revival, the boy was
nearly frantic. He could not eat or sleep and besought those
saints to tell him if he could obtain salvation. Some said flat
out what he'd *need* to do. Others begged to differ on just *how*
to do it. A handful hemmed and hawed as if it all came down
to *money*. He heard them out and thanked them, allowed they'd
been helpful and that he'd feel beholden to them all his days
on earth. He said that if, because of what they'd told him, and
with a little luck, he made it through the marbled portal, he'd
be sure to look them up and thank them once again. Enormous
in the pulpit, the preacher took his text on hell and warned
that wormy sinners were sure to wind up there and writhe in
boiling tar and beg for just one drop of water on the tongue,

but could not have it and would have to agonize forever, denied a split second of relief. When the first notes of the hymn of invitation quavered, the boy did not have second thoughts, but left his pew forthwith and hurried down the aisle to where the preacher stood with spacious arms outstretched as if they were the arms of Jesus—though he never made them out to be—and pled with the twitching boy, under much conviction, to fling himself into them and feel a letup of the sizzling in his loins that would not let him have a moment's peace. And further, with those sturdy arms beneath him, discover grace as cool and sweet as a dipperful of water from a hillside spring, now that heat was bearing down at its most ferocious. The boy, snatched straightaway from the devil's cauldron, looked back to where those sainted souls he vowed to emulate sat prim and proper in their pews and fanned themselves serenely, secure in knowing they had scored big-time in heaven, having borne true witness to what the love of God can do when it's put to the test, found equal to its promise. The boy, redeemed, was supremely happy, until the throes of manhood seized him and God came moseying around, giving notice that, having come into the world with brains, he was not exempt from using them and reminding him of numerous thorny questions he'd been pondering, but never once admitting to, since shedding boyhood and leaving it like September's snakeskin, when one's obliged to face up to the hoopla that happened years before, take inventory, and confront the heap of evidence that nothing of this earth will last forever, however durable it's said to be, and may not, truth be told, pull him through another winter or, for that matter, one more spring when April's certain to return, lighting candle-flares of redbud in dark cedars and calling into question what those old saints had told him when he was just thirteen, leading him to think that life would be his apple once he got in good with God Almighty.

Believing them, he'd fairly walked on water, convinced that what
he'd done would hold him, as in perpetuity, for ages everlasting.
Now he's learned the finest moments are the quickest gone,
that once of anything that feels good is never good enough, and
that assuming things are set to rights on the first try is nothing
but pure folly, certain to bring on the blues, and that one does
not as a rule throw the door of heaven open the first time he
yanks the latchstring. It is a massive door. But life's filled with
repetition, the endless circling of a wheel, and, in a love-jag, the
man the boy became will tote the cross of Jesus, until common
sense steps in and has its say in thunder: "Enough! You've been
at this for how long now? Don't you think it's time you walked
out, wide-eyed, into the light of intellect and stopped searching
for your face in mirrors with their aberrations, giving back
distorted images? So get up off your knees, and get a grip on
reason. A garden is the place for gourds. Your head's not one of
them, no matter what you were told back then. God's game for
questioning and brave enough to entertain your honest doubts.
He will not be tripped up, no matter what you ask him. He is an
old-school gentleman, and a scholar too. Pomposity is something
he abjures. Though he owns creation, he is the soul of modesty.
There's not a better landlord in all Kentucky. Kindness rules
him—*that* and the hand of mercy. He treats his people right."

THE TREE HOUSE

In late May of their fourteenth year, the two who thought
themselves as close as any brothers built a tree house high
among the branches of the largest oak, more than a century old,
in their upscale subdivision. When school was out, they tried
to beat the sun up every morning. Just as daybreak scattered
shards of light on rooftops, each boy quickly packed a lunch
and tried to be the first one at their secret place. Rain crows
called, as far away it seemed as manhood, even if there was not
a hint of rain. From their retreat, they could see the 18-wheeler
Peterbilts and hear their whining on the bypass that curved like
a quartermoon around the little town that served as a bedroom
community where thirty-somethings with new money, heading
up the corporate ladder, chose to get away from urban sprawl
and decadence. The boys caught snatches of the best of country
music playing on their neighbor's radio while, almost in the
nude, she soaked up rays all morning on her deck that was
thought to be secluded. And it *was* when looked at from street-
level, but was *not* to anyone who, concealed by a subterfuge of
trembly greenness, gazed down from the highest reaches of a
nearby oak. The boys were not into the Nashville Sound. It was
not their thing, not when being voyeurs was against the law and
by decency forbidden, but easily accomplished and such naughty
fun. One sneaked his dad's binoculars so they could study
her up close-up. The snakish hissing of the world seemed less
threatening to them in their arboreal refuge. A sibilance of leaves
smoothed out rough edges, muffled jagged sounds from down
below, made them less discordant. Throughout July, cooling
breezes singled out the tree for special courtesies and made it

seem as comforting as earth was apt to be. By the time August built up to a sizzle, they'd convinced themselves there was no way they could be apart. As evidence of it, they took a razor blade and mingled blood in boyhood's immemorial rite. They did not tell their parents why they wanted to, but finagled their consent to spend the muggy nights a little closer to the stars. But sensations they had recently begun to feel unsettled them. It seemed there were whispers in their blood. By Labor Day, the tree house was dismantled. Not a single board remained. When school began, classmates noticed that the boys were not like they'd been in May. They were edgy and went their separate ways. No one could have guessed which boy cried himself to sleep, while the other one stood below his window until well past midnight. What had happened *happened*, and could never be undone. Neither of them ever breathed a word of it.

AT THE RIVER

This is where the sainted ones forgather
when new believers are swathed by water
for the burial of sin. Here's where Jesus does
his thing, cleansing the penitents until a radiance
glows from within. They ascend into the rarefied air,
clad in the grace-stitched raiment of holiness,
stunned by how quickly their deliverance
was accomplished. Witnesses extend a hand
and quaver, "Shall We Gather at the River?"—
assigning glory where *they* think it belongs.
On other days in summer, especially when August
is a burning wound, farmhands steal an hour from their
toil, abandon fields, shuck off boots and jeans,
and reclaim their swimming hole when the manic
Christians are not using it.
                    But skinny-dipping is *not* baptism.
The would-be saints will not come to raise a prayer
or hymn, as if boys in their natural state might
somehow be impediments to grace, precluding
the approval a preacher's vivid gesture could bestow—
if one were anywhere in sight, and willing.
So who presumes to apprehend God's preference
for the uses of water?

SEERSUCKER

To all appearances, he was everything an upright citizen of
Canaan's Landing, the Delta town he lived in, ought to be. The
princely scion of judicious breeding and a family name beyond
reproach, he was heir to traits of character held to be impeccable.
And though he had old money, beaucoup in amount and
managed prudently, his demeanor on the street was lordly, all the
more for being absent ostentation. His mien was much observed
by nervous Nellies—men not without accomplishments of
note and good repute—whose mouths assumed an anus-shape
when they chanced to think of daughters, righteous in their
persons but fraught with plainness that rendered them in peril of
withering on the vine. No use, those men opined, in wondering
if *he* might consent to be such a daughter's suitor. They held out
little hope for that to happen, but were not above devising. He
could not stroll through those men's sprucy neighborhoods on
mint-green evenings without being hailed from deep verandas
where pitchersful of lemonade, newly squeezed, awaited him
untouched so that he might be the first one to partake in the
event he were to feel inclined. Invariably, he endured their not-
so-subtle invitations with his usual aplomb, and declined them
with a graciousness designed to mollify their disappointment
without discourtesy. The heat of summer in that region called
for seersucker, cool and crinkly, which he ordered from a pricey
clothier in Asheville. Being lithe as a dancer, the suit fitted him
like a sheath of wind. On Sunday mornings at St. Barnabas, he
slipped big bucks in the plate on the sly—thus quietly securing
his redemption for another week. With what facility did he meet
everyone's expectations of the ideal Southern gentleman—the

qualities of such a personage not being subject to dispute. What folks could not understand though was why he never, to *their* knowledge, cast a wishful eye toward marriage. The town was not without its bevy of assorted lovelies—each one guaranteed to have her hymen still intact and, therefore, qualified to be considered worthy for matters matrimonial. A classy wife was regarded as an asset at those social functions that a man of considerable distinction, such as he, was not easily forgiven for failure to attend. A couple of old college chums, well-wed, and not unmindful of their good fortune and their stations in banking and the law, were privy to his leaving town at midnight, on occasion, and heading up to Memphis. He'd been known to have a dalliance or two at Studs down by the bridge that crossed the Mississippi into Arkansas. The regulars who gathered there were quirky, into leather with accoutrements of whips and chains. Later, no one dared to mention that it was a leather bar where the skittish undertaker went to fetch him in his bloodied suit and rush him back to Canaan's Landing just before first light. The casket was kept closed, of course, and out of sight. He was hustled underground before any of his townsmen, save for one, knew that he was dead. There was never an investigation or any charges brought—well-bred people being mum, inimitably discreet.

E. Madelynne Muldraugh, Spinster

Of the favored Muldraugh sisters, all five of them
the crème de la crème of the upright Delta town
of Sweet Bethulia—greatly famed for its camellias
that brought folks from all over Mississippi
and parts of Alabama to admire them—
it was the middle daughter, E. Madelynne,
who was far less typical of the Southern Belle
in countless gothic novels than her mincing siblings.
(Regrettably, their papa, who'd been a widower
since his early manhood, had been shortchanged
in the course of his begetting: his loins
had withheld from him a son.)
Though she could be recalcitrant and unrepentant
and give her papa grief, E. Madelynne was never one
to mope about the house with an excruciating migraine
such as certain coddled Southern ladies
tend to get at their convenience.
Nor did she once take to her bed for days on end
with debilitating vapors because the wind
had unexplainably shifted to the east.
Neither did she loll on wicker, fanning with her best
embroidered handkerchief, lest a single droplet
of her sweat besmirch her person,
and thus preclude her being singled out for notice
by any of several high-toned gentlemen with old money
who strolled dapperly on Main Street
as if they owned the town.
E. Madelynne, endowed with far more strength

than beauty, was heady in her passions.
It was not within her nature to court serenity
or be the consort of contentment. Still, it was
a fearsome thing one April when that much-exalted lady
met her match in mirrors. It happened suddenly.
She espied what she took to be her spinsterhood approaching,
staring back at her from every mirror in the house.
By June, it seemed there was no place to hide.
The mirrors were conspiratorial. She convinced herself of it.
And so the formerly imperious E. Madelynne Muldraugh,
who had not subdued her tongue, or *tried* to,
was a broken woman, with her spirit shattered
and her nerves unstrung. Thus humbled and disconsolate,
she sought the ministrations of Reverend Chauncey Farkleberry,
the scholarly, unmarried pastor of her papa's church,
the Sweet Bethulia Baptist, which, since her earliest girlhood,
she'd sworn that she would never once attend.
She'd made it clear that, should the need
for churchly intercession ever seize her,
she'd seek one that was highbrow, such as the stately
Presbyterian with its costly stained glass windows
up on Main Street or, failing that, she'd take Communion
with the tightly wound Episcopalians whose ivied sanctum,
steeped in history, was at the end of Lawyers' Row.
She was in extremis, and she knew it.
Much to her chagrin, her face revealed her desperation.
She was reduced to making supplication,
entreating Reverend Farkleberry to join her
by appointment on her papa's deep veranda
on muggy evenings such as they were having
in the Delta at that time of year. And so it came
to pass that Reverend Chauncey Farkleberry

became the suitor and spiritual advisor, if not the soulmate,
of E. Madelynne Muldraugh—she once the talk
of Sweet Bethulia for openly disdaining organized religion,
refusing to abide by asinine conventions, and doing
what most folks in town would have liked to—
but lacked the courage. She heaped hot coals
on the heads of hypocrites. It had gotten to the point
that they would cross the street to avoid her, so abrasive
was she known to be. But she was the definition
of a lady nonetheless, everyone agreed, even those
who would be numbered among her enemies.
In spite of her misfortune, E. Madelynne was of high degree.
There were those with hearts not made of stone who,
while they felt no loss of love, were moved to pity
when they heard how she had been brought low
and was seeking solace from the Baptist minister.
They took no pleasure in her plight. If such a fate
could fix a person like E. Madelynne Muldraugh
in its sights, then they were not immune
from something worse befalling them. No one doubted
that the Reverend Chauncey Farkleberry was of fine intentions,
celibate, and devoid of guile. And his scruples
disallowed his having any penchant for indulgence
in what it had become apparent, to those experienced
in such matters, the twitching spinster direly needed.
The reverend's congregants agreed that his manhood
was not suspect and ascribed it to his calling.
But when Indian summer days with the antique look
of antimacassars covered every inch of Sweet Bethulia,
Reverend Chauncey Farkleberry and E. Madelynne
had their heads together in the shadowed privacies
of her papa's wide veranda. But that was not to last.

Nights were getting cold. Already there had been
a killing frost in the Upper South. Doughty maiden ladies,
brides, and gamey widows met at backyard fences
and allowed that, even in the Delta, winter could not be
long off. But there was rarely any mention
of the Muldraugh sisters, especially E. Madelynne who,
it was rumored, had gone into complete seclusion.
Reverend Chauncey Farkleberry was in his pulpit
every Sunday morning at eleven sharp. Nothing different
was discernible about him, but those evenings at E.
Madelynne's had taught him what his hands were well-suited
to accommodate. His finesse at delivering the sacrament to
deacons was something never seen before. And though his
sermons in no way betrayed the secrecies he'd come into
possession of, his tongue had learned refined maneuverings.
It was a feat much rarefied, an attribute of angels. He had
acquired it in the amber light, like Bible-glow, that had
made a shrine of E. Madelynne's veranda on those soulful
evenings. He found a new significance in the Song of Songs
no seminary in the land could have given him. There were
those in his congregation who were sure that when he rose
to preach, an inner light illuminated him from the core of
his soul, as if just he and God had sauntered off together for
a conversation no one else could have known about. And,
judging from his countenance, there was little likelihood
they ever would. There are things the tongue declines to
touch upon— they being far too holy for human utterance.
By Christmas Eve, folks in Sweet Bethulia learned that
death had come to call at the Muldraughs' door, and that
E. Madelynne had preferred immediate cremation over
anything as common as earth burial. During her last illness,
her sisters, greatly wroth, had pled with her not to give her

body to be so rapidly consumed, but to let the earth dandle it a while. Their beseeching was to no avail. She'd paid no attention to a word they said. Distraught, they took leave of her chamber, wringing their hands and weeping as if they'd been entreating one already dead. She burned divinely and with vigor—her writhing reminiscent of erotic pleasures the undertaker said, when he brought her ashes home. The ecstasy it afforded him was fraught with palpitations of a weakened heart. It was told by some who were privy to the plans that E. Madelynne's memorial service would be like none that anyone was used to, or preferred. Nor would it start a trend the town would be obliged to get the hang of. So at the time appointed, an invited handful assembled at Sweet Bethulia's Garden of Perpetual Repose. They found Reverend Chauncey Farkleberry instructive more for what he did *not* say than what he did. That the man was in decline, enfeebled by the loss of E. Madelynne, was evident. Some thought he'd never make it through the eulogy, but his heart was set on a culminating statement which he managed to deliver with a mixture of mystery and mischief that was titillating, but provided little in the way of illumination. He set his gaze on what to everyone was invisible above the bare-boned trees. His tones induced a vast, collective shiver in the folks forgathered: "If it will quell your curiosity," he began, "I will speak of what you might term slight indecencies that you fain would hear about or perish. You thought you knew E. Madelynne Muldraugh—even had the temerity to call her one of you. I regret to tell you that you are much mistaken. You see, it was not so long ago that her compliant body with those sculpted limbs became to no one's eyes but hers deserving of an adulation hitherto denied her since here in Sweet Bethulia there seems to be a dearth of gentlemen who, by virtue of selective breeding, are cognizant of beauty such as those connoisseurs in ancient Athens—they who made of it an obsession that consumed them utterly. With what ease, but how intrepidly, among complacencies of peacock feathers, arising from her bath each evening, E. Madelynne indulged her darkest fantasies. A fever not of earth had seized her. She was more ravenous than Eve after her encounter with the fabled serpent. Our lady cast aside her reason and her morals too. Though I was there ostensibly to interpose between E. Madelynne and her demons should things become too quirky, too untidy—and shepherd her to biblical injunctions, having to do with heaven, it soon became apparent that I, the one entrusted with her soul, had become obscenely overwrought and could not conceal it. Suffice it to say that, with impunity, E. Madelynne and I plunged headlong into a ravishment we mortals are not entitled to. It was tornadic; no doubt alarming to departed saints—and sent them scurrying as if they were a padarack of guineas. Do not grieve for E. Madelynne and think that she departed earth unfulfilled, dissatisfied. In spite of what her mirrors may have told her, the lady did not go unrequited and deprived. She was cremated like she liked it long before she died." On a January evening, Reverend Chauncey Farkleberry left the Delta on the westbound train. He carried with him only what his worn valise would hold—no destination given, and none asked for. A trifle ostentatiously, the season of camellias came again to Sweet Bethulia. And people went about their business—better off for what they did not know.

J. Ethelbert Foppish Goes to Church

Ever so fastidious, his habiliments agreeably designer, his
accoutrements complete with a gold-knobbed cane and his
ancestral pocket watch with its ornate fob, he is disdainful
of common folk he meets and will not greet them as he
proceeds along the Delta town's Main Street to visit God.
The Sabbath bell competes with fluted birdsong for his
notice, but he is disinclined to increase his pace, finding
haste beneath him— a behavior most unsightly. Well-
heeled for life with passed-down money, he is intolerant of
those on government relief his town is overrun with. (He
thinks of what the Bible says about the poor.) He enters
St. Bartholomew's and genuflects beside his pew just as the
priest commences. He remembers that he did not bring
his Book of Common Prayer, and he's never taken time
to learn a word of the liturgy by heart. He simply *must*
do better, he opines, before whatever time's already been
appointed for his dying. Just to be safe, he aims never to
leave home without his nitroglycerin— the tiny bottle in
his pocket. But this morning, busily preening, he quite
forgot to put it there. All of a sudden, pains pummel his
chest, his arms throb to his fingers. He grows limp, goes
down, crumples on the kneeler as they pass the Peace. Not
one soul notices. They assume he's praying.

In August, a Solitary Farmer in the Backcountry Ponders the Meaning of Life, What the Hereafter's Like, and the Exact Location of Heaven

His crops are laid by, and he has time on his hands.
August is a boil on his spirit. No surgeon's lancet
lets the pus out. The boil gets larger, skankier.
This month has no mercy on the living or the dead.
There comes a moment in these onerous days
that's no less unnerving than the instant when a dapper
undertaker steps forward and shuts a coffin lid for good.
Old hymns like "Hark, I Hear the Harps Eternal"
and "When I Can Read My Title Clear" provide cold comfort.
He remembers the revivals of his boyhood when he used to hear
the folks who were his kin belting out Southern gospel,
getting on a jag for Jesus. He wishes he could hear them
singing still. But he settles for a mourning dove's
cedar-cloistered chant most any afternoon.
That other sound he hears, almost inaudible,
when he scans the slow burn of sky for a hint of rain
can only be the clocktick of the cosmos all around him—
the *everywhere* and *everything* as close as his right hand,
and yet as far away as someone he once loved, now a long time
underground in the Deep Creek churchyard. If the heaven
he wants to believe in is someplace in the sky, he wonders
what could be its exact location and dimensions. Nothing gives
him a clue. One's ingress there happens instantaneously, so he's
been told, when the soul takes leave of the body's last breath
and, delivered from its fragile link to tedious mortality, shows up

bleary-eyed in the anteroom adjoining paradise.
That wouldn't be so bad, he thinks.
The pestilence of dog days is unheard-of there,
as is the mirror's aberration and the cupped palm's
maddening tendency to hold out the promise of release,
but deliver regret. He thinks he's been forgiven of youthful
and recent indiscretions. But a sinister edge to the wind
tells him no man can merit redemption
and that this is no time to be playing hide-and-seek
with any stranger from the other side who claims to be
a savior; no time to look askance at what the Bible says,
though still unproven. This is the devil's weather
when the faithful doubt their prayers make it to the rooftop
of the meetinghouse, much less the ear of God.
More than in all other months, he knows he's alone
in a universe that flaunts its snake-eyed indifference.
Why should a man not slit his throat when the revenant light
imbues these breath-held afternoons the color of grief?
To him, life's meaning is spittle in the dust. But, to be safe,
he clings to a remnant of his early faith as if it might
stand him in good stead with angels, though privately
he thinks it's most unlikely he'll encounter any.
He halfway suspects they are creatures of mankind's frantic
devising, and the human refusal to be ruled by logic.
He tries to imagine the New Jerusalem, and wonders
if it might not be the centerpiece of legend
instead of an actual place where August, like a low-grade
fever that wears the spirit down, cannot get in and do
its yearly mischief. The preacher told him grace is free,
even to the scrawny loiterer in Gethsemane
who never sleeps but does his share of watchful waiting.
Though there's scant evidence this is the case, he holds

out hope that when the hard day's almost done
and the end is only a breath-catch or two away,
Jesus, who's been rumored to have risen from the dead and
ascended into heaven, will come and ferry him
across the fabled Jordan to those longed for fields
of light the old ones sang about—
the inscrutable landscape of forever.

The Young Preacher Kneels at the Mourners' Bench of the Cowskill River Baptist Church before the August Revival

What truth this aged wood signifies we have not the grace to
comprehend, but here in the backcountry where my frenzied
boyhood took its toll it is August and the full moon savages the
red-necked children of the Lord, constraining them to writhe
and moan, contorted on a rack of emotions

never to be understood. Lookers-on would fear that when such
frantic penitents get to going good, they might pierce their
foreskins with the spikes Christ hung from on Golgotha's cross.
After long travail, an orgiastic snap robs them of their common
sense and rids them of every shred of reason.

From a turbulence of scarlet, mistaken for his blood, they
emerge disconsolate, and fling themselves with piteous abandon,
like sacks of salt, on the mercy seat— their faces wan, distorted
out of shape, and their glazed eyes cold as Arctic ice. Though I'm
not disposed to be irrational, I have extremities of my own to
suffer,

for I too—I made a covenant with anonymity when the two-
faced dusk and hot staccato rhythms of a backstreet dive invited
my indulgence in a variety of sins with assorted sinners. Thus
undone by lust and shame, I knew I would be driven to this
clapboard meetinghouse I grew up in, where once, in a beautiful
silence,

a call came to me across the vastness of arboreal distance like a
mourning dove's. The old upright and the rough-hewn pews may
echo groans in my imaginings of those I loved who would not
be chastened—nor could they turn away from pleasures of the
body, just as I could not. Now I know that acts of kindness

have availed me nothing. Though, with fives and tens, I've
greased the palms of strangers faking hunger when they were
craving booze. The pocket change that I've doled out to urchins
will not utter one syllable in my behalf—nor will food I've
carried to the doors of widows, recently bereaved, and the
fatherless.

Summer's guilt's a downer. It douses groin-fire, quivering
like heat lightning on the sharpened dirks of feverish nights.
Unwisely, I had hoped that mercy could be bought with what's
been known to *pass* for love in rented rooms, even though I
know that love itself can be elusive, seen dimly as a sun dog.

I was Sunday-schooled in the gospels well. But, surly, given to
recalcitrance, I was intent on proving that the elders I was taught
to heed were hopelessly befuddled. No longer teenaged-arrogant,
I ghost through tangled yearnings, repenting of my youthful
indiscretions and ashamed of making sport of truth's

simplicity. It is a country wisdom that suffices me, and I'm
obliged to tell it: salvation has its price and makes of night an
ally; the birds of darkness stir, make psalms among the moon-
flecked leaves, and foxes take a cue from wind, double back, and
frustrate hounds in fields of mist, white as Queen Anne's lace;

arousing from his posture by her side, the bridegroom visits love upon his bride; in country graveyards, the newly dead, spending their first night underground, are insomniac. Keeping watch in his galactic tree house, God declaims in syllables of light, *"Under my wings you may abide forever. There is no certainty but this."*

The Widow

What was to be her life must have happened,
she thinks, without her noticing,
when she was cooking supper for her young
husband, rocking heat-fretful babies, canning
produce from her garden all those end-of-summer
afternoons, or sitting hour after hour
with her ailing mother, whose death crown
she now keeps under glass in her closed-off parlor.
She starts taking time apart and studying it
in increments: months, years, decades.
That's when she remembers those early birthdays—
the chocolate cake, the brand-new half dollar
under her upside-down plate when they called her
to the table. The year she married, her husband picked
wildflowers and held them behind his back
when he came in from the field for dinner.
Just a little something, he would have called them
if she'd made a big to-do over wildflowers
on her birthday.
She knew how far he'd gone to pick them
after topping tobacco all morning. Too soon he left her,
just as middle age set in— the children
grown and moved away. Ever since, she's had time
on her hands for puttering around a house
too large for her. But even now she cannot bring
herself to leave it and move into a condo.
Pink and yellow roses nodding
on the backyard trellis stay in bloom for her

until the fall's first killing frost each year.
Sometimes as dusk falls, she tries to call to mind
those other summers, but rarely does a remnant
of a single day appear. Though she's been a widow
almost half her life, she's never been unfaithful
in either thought or deed. She visits his churchyard
grave every Sunday after the service.
Kneeling before his stone, she says his name
over and over with her finger. It makes her happy.
The only part of her life, she knows, that mattered to her
happened when she was younger,
all those summers ago.

To Henry Thoreau at the Autumnal Equinox

And so, Henry, kinsman of my spirit, you've been gone since
early May of a year I was not here to see. They tell me it was
right at nine o'clock in the morning when you took your leave.
The earliest apple trees were leafing and greening as they always
do on that day every year. Still do. Strange how that happens.
It's always baffled me. Most of the villagers, when they heard
the news, went about the streets in mourning, even if they never
knew what to make of you. Your closest friends conversed,
agreed, and threw you a funeral at the church—it mattering not
to them you'd never entered it. Lordly Mr. Emerson delivered
quite a eulogy. To be exact, he *pontificated* most all afternoon.
Some folks, tired of sitting, squirmed more than they were
wont to during Sunday meeting. They meant no disrespect. You
would not have minded. Besides, by that time, you were out of
range and couldn't hear your best friend send you off with such
a plethora of verbal flourishes. You'd no doubt reached some
cosmic destination. I would imagine that this little village was
the last thing on your mind. Other precincts of the universe had
sat you down to supper. Though never much for talking when
you were alive, I suspect you regaled those folks with an account
of how you put gloves on Lidian's chickens. And I'd guess
someone asked about the night when you set Concord on its
ear by going to jail rather than paying your taxes to help finance
a war you found immoral. Undoubtedly someone brought up
Transcendentalism and urged you to define it, and explain what
it meant to you.

      Down here, Henry, a single clocktick has just
let another summer go. It's fall again. Surely you remember

how you loved the tang and tree-shine of our New England autumns. But you loved spring and summer too—the seasons of growing things and the manner of their growing. I still think the piece you wrote about wild apples is among your best. It took nature's own apostle to write such as that. If you were to return here—a youthful revenant— you'd find no decent wildflowers in the fields surrounding Concord for Louisa and your Aunt Sophia. Toward the end of August, most everything except the pesky weeds got sickly-looking and, in no time at all, was dead, withered as a mummy. If you remember, that's the way it is each year when that end-of-summer light begins to look far-flung and starts subsiding. And there's a keening sound, sad as any funeral hymn, that makes us think the dead are calling our names again. But it's only the wind, nothing but that hot, late-summer grieving of the wind. If the weather keeps in sync with how it's been in other years, we'll get a killing frost early in October. By the way, Walden Pond's a mess. It would sicken you. The summer tourists took their toll, but meant no harm. Now it's been defiled by all sorts of vagrants, malcontents and scoundrels claiming to be your *disciples*. Horse feathers! If you ask me, they're everything *but*. The place has been muddled by discarded reefer-wrappers, rock concert tickets torn in half, crunched-up beer cans and soggy condoms—foul things you wouldn't want to look at.

Now I'm obliged to ask if, anywhere in that galactic thicket, flowering with stars, you've met up with what Mr. Emerson calls the Universal Mind, the Oversoul, the great I AM? And if so, were you chastised soundly for not showing much concernment for your soul when you were traipsing through the woods alone, and exploring rivers with your brother, John, instead of studying the Holy Writ, memorizing verse after verse of Genesis and Deuteronomy? Being the way he is, Mr.

Emerson will want to know, not that it will matter much to him. He pretty much abandoned all that when he left the pulpit. Now he and Bronson Alcott and Louisa May get together and have such conversations that would befuddle minor gods. Lidian makes no bones about not understanding all they're saying. And so she does the wise thing and keeps mainly to herself. More often than she'd like, it occurs to her she doesn't know the man she's married to. She knows his intellect takes precedence, and it's the new idea he's yet to have that he values above most people, and that includes her. Did you know he considered *you* his only equal and that he loved you as much as one man can love another man, even if he never told you? It's true, and you should be aware of it, even if belatedly.

But enough about everyone's Mr. Emerson and his intellect. Sound carries farther and more clearly on most autumn nights. So we should hear your footfalls when you climb icy altitudes past Orion to worlds undreamt of that Hubble, voyaging alone, is apt to see close-up. A poet from the century just past wrote something I will close with, leave with you. He wrote, "It is the human season on this sterile air." I think the human season rids the heart of its old debris. I do not think you'll disagree.

(The words in quotes are from "Immortal Autumn" by Archibald MacLeish.)

A Killing Frost

Each year in June, her vaunted roses flaunt their opulence
on the front yard trellis, climbing upward, higher, until
they're luminous with the light of heaven. They are unspoken
parables, beatitudes made visible, in the mornings, in the
afternoons. Come evening, they are reverend as plainsongs
and old hymns. Sometimes when the moon is full, she goes
out and stands beside them, and thinks they show as much
of holiness as earth is apt to know. She tells a friend or two
about them—no more than that. For she is modesty itself,
demure, retiring. She seems to give no thought to any season
other than the one at hand, now that summer's lush, solstitial
in the Cumberlands, the only place she's known as home all
her sixty-seven years.

One evening fifty years ago—and it was summer
then—she was a comely girl when her first chance at love
came calling. But her papa, too possessive, unable to conceal
his disapproval, met the young man, brandishing his
revolver, steely, steady in his hand. It was not loaded. But
it was enough. Word traveled fast and, as might have been
expected, no other would-be suitor ever once came near her.
Her heart was broken, but no one saw her shed a tear. She
did not give up hoping. She cut out scraps from dresses,
dusters, her papa's outworn shirts, even feed sacks. Almost
every day, and far into the night in winter, she made quilts,
beautiful beyond compare. Hers were the neatest stitches in
the county, everyone agreed. The quilts, she thought, would
be useful to a newly wedded couple on those frigid nights

when drafts, wind-driven, got indoors and caused a chill throughout the house though extra logs were heaped on fires kept going in the stoves and fireplace. She was fooling no one but herself, and she knew it. If extra quilts were piled on any bed, it would be her own—the Jenny Lind in which she slept alone, and had since girlhood and would continue to until the only bridegroom she could count on would be sure to make of her his bride.

She did not hate her papa, knowing he had doted on her since the night his Millie died in childbirth He had not turned against the ways of men with women. He'd been young himself once and remembered how, not infrequently, he'd visited himself upon a bevy of young ladies who were never quite themselves afterward: some of them felt all but murderous when he chose Milicent, whom he deemed the fairest, whose place he would have taken in her dying moment if God had paid attention to his prayers. He never meant to give his daughter grief. But he could not help but notice as she took on that *look* of a settled spinster, the kind of look that hints of some severity of heart, though she was well-regarded in the county for her gentleness and pleasing ways. The year it *happened*, he had no way of knowing that she'd seen summer come and go one time too many. When October flared, she watched the weathercock arrow to the north and stay there, and knew that cold fronts out of Canada would put an end to her surviving roses, still ablaze in vivid pinks and reds and yellows as if it were no later than July or early August in the Cumberlands. Long back, before September, katydids had foretold an early frost. She could not keep from smiling when she went into the attic, took the pistol from a trunk. Contrary to her papa's notion, she did not grieve for roses, though she loved them and would have had them stay in bloom even when the trellis sagged beneath the weight of late December's snows. The chill that had gotten in the marrow of her bones had come out of season on a summer evening half a century before—when her papa met the boy and warned him in language not intended to be subtle that he'd risk losing life and limb if he set foot inside the front yard gate.

American Autumn

Late sunflares die out in the Rappahannock,
the Shenandoah and the French Broad
and the rivers darken; slow subtleties of weather

heap iceblink-blue of October afternoons
into corpse-gray ashes of November's sky,
God's wintry shadow on Nebraska

Clouds of garrulous crows forgather
among crazed gravestones, regard blurred epitaphs
and blurt out dire predictions in Burnt Church, Tennessee

An impious mischief of winds in Amarillo
chills Flat Rock and Cullowhee to the marrow,
bruits rumors of snow approaching Barnstable,

frost-bruises Eufaula's last heirloom roses
and frets first light's filigree on the tallish
Victorian windows of Waxahachie

Soon the Blue Northers will roll across the Dakotas
and put the Big Muddy on notice
it's in for its share of the tough love of ice

In southeastern Kentucky, the Cumberlands
are e-mailing Ecclesiastes
across all known time zones, past light-years

to someone who could be in the back unknown of cyberspace
beyond viny constellations like fox grapes
where some think Genesis could begin again

I start a fire, pour coffee in the mug with Thoreau's
handwriting on it, put on Barber's "Adagio for Strings"
and let the grave splendor of the music master me

In my imaginings, you are in the next room writing a poem

October Elegy for One Who Died
in Another October

In Memoriam: H. D. C.

I was thirteen the wind-grieved night you died in a city you had
rarely been to, if at all. Now that you've been gone for decades
into some permanence where our wispy Indian summers go
for good, an underland conversant with the course of seasons,
giving ground to that final season of the long forgetting, I am
here where remembrance is strong around me like the cloying
smell of too many overripe persimmons. If I could, I would tell
you how things in this new century are up to nothing good.
Take my word for it. You would not feel at home in this world
that I call *addled*. I call it that because no other word will do.
Nothing is like it used to be when you were alive in that country
place with its run-down clapboard farmhouse and a few scrawny
roses on the backyard fence that made summer beautiful for
you. I'm free now to say I found nothing beautiful about it. I
remember how it droned on and on into what seemed to be the
never-ending, and how your nubby roses hung on into fall. They
were dwarfish, short on virtue, little short of being laughable,
whereas the neighbors gloried in an opulence of antique roses,
nodding in their elegance on princely trellises. I was but a half-
pint boy the day you told us you'd be going soon. I didn't know
how soon you meant by *soon*. And going soon to *where?* It was
a God-freighted moment when your words weighted down my
shoulders like gunny sacks chock-full of swarthy, firmly-fleshed
potatoes, with their pungent earth-smell, we'd only finished
digging and storing in the cellar the afternoon before. When

they got me out of bed one night and told me that, decimated by an exotic fever your doctors thought you'd brought back from that Pacific war, your numbness had finally found your heart and killed you, I was gravestone-mute but thought I was too big for tears. My ears belied the real: each clocktick seemed to be a hammer-blow on steel. I hated you for dying. I hated all those faces changing shapes and sizes in the too-warm room. It was unnatural—that second summer. Outside the open window, insects kept on rehearsing their insidious music, full of an Ives-like dissonance that showed no signs of letting up. Your family had been told there'd be no taking you inside the church. The fear of what had killed you allowed only the briefest graveside service early the next morning—and no time wasted as those soldiers, forgoing ceremony, hustled your sealed military casket underground. I remember thinking how that woman poet in my American lit book got it right: *life goes on though good men die,* even when we do not think it can, even if we do not think we want it to. But days and seasons pass, and other years bring us other reasons for being glad to see Octobers go. Now, I'm on the knife blade's edge of being threescore years and ten—all the Bible has allotted me. Beyond that, everything's on loan. I saw young manhood come and go like a rained-out July carnival, that couldn't take the time to hang around, but had to get a move on to the next scheduled town and it seems now that the better part of my adulthood happened when I did not take the mirror at its word. It's pointless to wonder where those good years went and, for that matter, whatever happened to what seemed to be a thousand nights of apples right for plucking in the orchard, no farther than a stone's throw from your kitchen door. If I could be certain you would hear me, I'm fairly sure that I would try to tell you how much it meant, just being there with you. Our friendship was not an April and November screwup of frazzled

memory's making, but something rare that *happened*, subsumed
forever in an autumn mix of mist and stone. You have no way
of knowing it, but I still see your clammy garden that, each year,
became more difficult to tend, a patchwork of scraggly vegetables
on worn-out land, hard as hearts sometimes get when they are
denied one time too many. Being so young back then, I could
not have known that I would miss you more than some I *thought*
I loved—since you were simply there, someone I took for
granted, someone to sit down at the table with for three square
meals a day. What bitter schooling these decades of your absence
have been. Now that I'm twice as old as you were when you
died, I can finally remember what I never would have thought
to tell you. But I would not call you back now when trees are
moping, shrugging off their leaves. Would it mean anything if
I were to say what needed saying years ago? Or has the mercy
of your grave's ineffable solicitude taught you that being dead is
largely a serene indifference to the living? Have you lain there
over half a century not caring that when the last of your apples
are picked each year in old October's blaze and blur, I find it
harder to remember how you looked and spoke, yet mourn you
more?

Raking Leaves on All Saints' Day

for E. G. S.

This year, the day the church calls holy falls on a Sunday.
It is filled with a huddle of presences keeping distance:
some of them familiar, though most are not.
Done in sepia, the earth is static, drowsing—
not in an ambience of summer, but in its pale illusion.
No matter if we'd like to take our ease on the deep porch
and contemplate this day, what it means for us,
and for those revenants who've come back
from the never-ending, and what their coming means,
the leaves knee-deep on the lawn need heaping.
Cloistral, biding its time, twilight holds its breath,
fragile as a fish scale vase. Somewhere there's the pealing
of a vesper bell, its tones, cool pearls, reminding us
that years ago there were flights of spirit-birds circling
the spire of a subterranean chapel on a shrouded hill.
We gather armloads of the pungent leaves and place them
in a potpourri. Our veins unreel godhead backward,
animate the fire of nerve-net glory and the pulse of grace.
We hone our words, say this wineskin full of vintage weather
will not hold, we are in for days as poisonous as hemlock,
the long range forecast predicts an early snow.
With luck, and the prayers of the haggard faithful
most men will make it to a state of bliss. The first night
of November commences its descent, a providential sleight
of hand. Just as the leaves are bagged, placed curbside,
the muted benediction of darkness closes out the day.

Walt Whitman in Camden, Autumn 1890

Now take that picture there by the stairway, for instance.
Because he loves me, Tom Eakins never would have painted me
looking woebegone or sickly. He knows I've got my pride and do
not want to be remembered as anything but old-man-studly. You
say that few will remember me? Ah, more than just a few. You'll
see. Bucke says there's no doubt about it, and he's the one who
ought to know. He was here for days on end picking my brains
when he was working on the book about me. I discouraged it.
I told him that no one sane would lay out hard-earned cash for
it, not when the good stuff has been bruited about from mouth
to ear—peddled everywhere there was a mortal soul to hear.
But, to my amazement, the townsfolk made a run on stores
and snatched it up the minute that it hit the shelves. They can't
get enough, it seems to me. They say that I'm a man of some
intrigue here in dreary Camden. *Dreary* is the word. It's that, I
grant you. Folks used to look to me for whatever juicy morsel
they could get their tongues around. I've seen them hunched
behind their hands when I strolled on the streets come evening.
Nowadays, I can't oblige them. As for boys from the working
class, my name got linked with theirs improperly, though I do
not deny I loved them. Though some, I suppose, would have
called it infatuation that I'd convinced myself was love. But just
imagine me, getting myself all bothered up over their supple
bodies. And I confess I did. I did it often. Just something in my
nature made it so I couldn't help myself. But, in time, something
intervened—call it God's sweet grace— so that what I felt got
tedious, became insufferable, and finally left me with my wits
intact. I'm aware my name did not come out unsullied in the

eyes of those self-righteous folk who are quick to judge, ready
with their low opinions. It doesn't matter. Time's unmanned me.
All I am is old and bedfast now and can't hold my water like
I should. I'm obliged to be discreet as best I can, like particles
of dust around the doily on my nightstand. The perturbations
of the flesh are no bother anymore. My cock's as flaccid as a
twice-killed snake. Still, on my good days, I'm an old charmer.
I could coax a choir of crows to sing the Shaker hymns and
sound like a treeful of mockingbirds. But I've got no one
fooled, especially those who come to visit. They can see that I'm
unwell. I go as often as the weather will allow to see the tomb
I'm having built for papa, mama, and the boys, as well as for
myself. I'm fearful it won't be ready by the time that one of us
has need of it. Lately I've dreamed of Mr. Lincoln's ghost always
prowling Washington's backstreets instead of staying put in that
Springfield tomb with him. Did anyone tell you that I wrote an
elegy for him in lilac-weather after Booth's pistol-gust stopped
the play that night at Ford's? Some say it's sure to be in every
child's schoolbook in the land. Maybe so, I'd not prevent it, but
I suspect that such as that will be a long time coming. All I know
for sure is that it's late and I must get my rest. You wouldn't
think I'd say this, but now it comforts me to know that when
I wake tomorrow morning, there'll be no boy sprawled asleep
beside me. Let passersby pass by. I've seen enough boys' bodies to
do me for a lifetime. Count on it. My latchstring will not be out
tonight.

Jasper Johns' *Map*

It doesn't happen often now, but there are still times when
I can feel your body fitted to mine in the bed-raptness
of a November night twenty-something years ago. All of
a sudden, you said, "This is not the first time I've done
this." I said, "I know"—and there was a long pause. "I
know," I said again, and turned toward the wall. Above
me, Jasper Johns' *Map* glowed, disquieting as foxfire in
the room's semidarkness. All the states of America bled
into a crazed collage of colors. No wonder a mischief of
winds in western Oklahoma could stir up trouble halfway
across the country; no wonder

the Susquehanna roiled to flood stage in the
Cumberlands, and New England's achy gravestones
wailed their blurred epitaphs miles to the south in Burnt
Church, Tennessee. All night I listen to the idiomatic
wheel-talk of long freights slowing down to a throaty
crawl through this measly nowhere town in the Upper
South. The murmured rumors of winter bruising Grand
Forks, North Platte, and Missoula are bruited about our
tall Victorian windows. I stay tuned to classic country
streaming from Amarillo. There are times I think I'd
swear that Willie Nelson

says your name over and over, crooning "You Were
Always on My Mind," while a mean piano and a steel
guitar get to going good like a Blue Norther moving
through. But this poem's not about that. All this time, it's

been trying to untangle knotted snarls of words and stitch them to the syntax of that *other* night. I remember how I lay there, sleepless, imagining a smooth stranger making love to you. I know I should be over it. But if I could see you, if I could talk to you, I'd have to ask you, "Why did you tell me? Why did you have to ruin that night for me?"

THE NOVEMBER VISITOR

Strangest thing. Strangest kind of wonder. How people like you,
lacking consideration, can disappear for a couple of decades and
more, with not so much as a card to say you're alive or dead, and
then show up out of nowhere when November's here. Why does
a person do that? You have no answer. But it does not surprise
me, your standing here—no ghost or revenant or spectre. Your
being here must have something to do with the earth getting
colder, and lonesome-sounding, grinding on its axis this time
of year. Come to think of it, the world is lonely—and not just
lonely-sounding. I noticed there's been ax-fall and crow-call in
my neighbor's woods all day. Made me think how soon winter's
coming. It's on its way here even as I speak. And just this week,
the last V of wild geese arrowed south toward the Gulf. That's
always a sign. Now that we're on slow time it's a pale five o'clock
of hound-cry. Just before you came, the Full Beaver Moon,
like an orb of frost, was poised, cock-like, yonder on the east
horizon. Reminds me, it's time to start a fire for supper, turn on
a lamp or two. Don't think my hospitality's gone south, and that
I'm being rude if I stop talking long enough to check out the
news and weather on TV. (It's my routine now.) My life's mostly
how I like it, fairly even-keeled. After what happened—what was
it?— twenty-something years ago, I've expected no miracles, and
there've been none. This is a far cry from that other November. I
was younger, and burning, then. That was another world. Don't
get me wrong. It's not that I mind your happening by. Or did
you come here for a reason, something on the order of the one
you had before? If so, forget it. Since you were here, I've taken
at least two dozen calendars off the wall at year's end and put up

new ones. The mantel clock's kept track of tedious minutes and
added them up into even more tedious hours. I'd say I've had
enough time to get used to your absence, wouldn't you? One
thing's sure. I don't need to drink from your *wineskin of mercy*—
wasn't that what you called it? Instead of a strong libation, this
time around I'll keep my head clear with coffee. Has it occurred
to you I'm getting older? And you're no longer young. So we'll
spend the evening at my kitchen table with the ash tray running
over between us while the cold constellations of late autumn
spread light-years on the far side of creation, like vines loaded
down with fox grapes, luminous as finger lamps. One thing
more I'll tell you. Most nights, I'm asleep on the couch by nine.
It's as good a place as any for a man alone. You can take my bed.
It's not been turned down for longer than I can call to mind. It's
time it was. By you.

OLD 100TH

It is an end of Indian summer sound: the ice-blue
of a late November sky that modulates into a minor,
gray as the ashes of a body that was loved. It is the
tinge of yellow in the pale farewell of misty light,
and leafsmoke's scriptural ascent toward heaven
from a patchwork of small town yards—this other
Sabbath's liturgy, this annual rite predictable as the
harsh voice-over of a single crow, preceding autumn's
imminent departure. The deep bass notes of the first
hard freeze and the hint of early snow are in this old
doxology. A severe music cast in strict New England
measures, its wintry tones align with bare-limbed
gratitude for earth and firmament, praising fox grapes
ripe on viny constellations, and Orion's mighty stride.

Bright Canaan

Wondrous fair, the shape notes invest the stoic air
with radiance. The Holy Spirit descends on snowy
pinions, and the old clapboard meetinghouse becomes
susurrous. Suddenly, there is another rustling sound,
this one different from the first. We look around and,
lo, it is he—Christ—who moves among the rustic pews
where, work-haggard, their hands like dried-up leather,
our pale ancestors hold worn hymnals. The words of
"Hark, I Hear the Harps Eternal" lilt like myriad sparks
toward the anteroom of the never-ending. How the
jubilant hymn delights the ear of God as he observes
another Sabbath's bending of the knee. See how he spins
out his grace like a spider on progenitor and descendant
alike. Someone, a willowy maiden in the back row,
rises to a descant. The hymn, resonant in the mouths
of dead sopranos, ascends on the sun-charged wings
of morning toward where the angels wait to receive it,
make it their own, and sing it in those aerial pavilions.

December Night

There's no new Nativity in the making, no antsy teenage couple
heading toward a jerkwater town—he, no titled scion, nudging
a donkey along, and she, no daughter of fortune, holding on,
"heavy with child," as they said back then, her pregnancy of
dubious origin, sorely trying any thinking man's belief. There are
no fat-cat Persian potentates, no scholars to the manor born, no
tycoons revving up the engines of their private jets for a flight in
tandem westward, risking being blown to bits over Iraq's killing
fields. No longer are there shepherds anywhere in sight, putting
up with boredom and the vagaries of weather on Judaean hills.
They learned there's no future in it. No stunned astronomers
are peering at a newfound star, hitherto undreamed of, that
Hubble's tracked in space, an unsuspected luminary brighter
than any seen before—breaking news repeated ad nauseam on
CNN. Angels are all the rage, big sellers now. They come in all
conceivable styles and sizes, and some of them are pricey. You
see them on everything from bookmarks to trivets—and, of
course, the obligatory greetings we still send to people we hardly
know anymore. As for music, there's no ethereal descant above
a stable anywhere— not in Bethlehem, and not in Kentucky. So
this year, like all the times before, it's Luke who'll set us straight,
as if the gospel-glow of stained glass windows, candlelight, and
carols by a country choir were not enough: the Nativity we have,
the only one there will be, happened near a feed trough in a
makeshift shelter where livestock were bedded down one night
in December two millennia ago.

CHRISTMAS EVE

The earth, after several hard freezes in a row, is ready to accommodate the heavy snow the weatherman predicted on the newscast at 6 o'clock. As far back as late September, *The Old Farmer's Almanac* told us this would happen. Directly overhead, the full moon of Advent is close to bursting. The moonwash illuminates the hills and bottomland for miles around. Distant farmhouses—century-old two-storied clapboard and new low-slung ranch style—are wrapped in strings of blinking lights, inviting any travelers, a man and wife, say—and she with child—who, far from home and cold and hungry, might be out this late. They could warm themselves and share a cornucopia of food at any farmer's table.

On Deep Creek Hill, the Baptist bell, stock-still, holds back its hallelujahs. The church is dark now and getting cold. Earlier, we had candle-glow and carols by a country choir, the prayers of the faithful, and the story of the Lord's Nativity retold. Afterward, we who heard it went out, sad, into the night, steadying our candles, knowing Peace on Earth is still a hollow phrase on Christmas cards, the rattle of a gourd, and nothing more.

Westward, the sky banks low and starts to bulge into an overhang of snow-clouds. Old barns loom spectral, shaping rectangular shadows on the landscape. Each one could be Bethlehem's stable, preparing for a miracle at midnight. There is the shuffling of animals, anxious in their stalls. They sense the annual visitation of shepherds, wise men, and a host of angels. In the distance, house by house, the lamps in windows are turned off. Soon Santa Claus will be along. He was seen on radar, crossing the Canadian border into North Dakota at 8 o'clock. They told it on a TV bulletin at 10, and children headed straightaway to bed. Come morning, snow will be falling, carloads of kinfolk will be coming out from town, and on Deep Creek Hill there'll be the glorious commotion of the Baptist bell.

The Young Preacher's First Christmas Eve Sermon to the Congregation of the Cowskill River Baptist Church

Good friends—and you *are* my good friends!—it has pleased
God to send me here to tell you what I know. The four
Gospels we rely on do not plug up all the holes. Therefore, the
narrative is sketchy; by no means is everything spelled out, the
fabric neatly stitched, thus disallowing all sensible conjecture.
Everything's not cut and dried and every hard-nosed doubter
satisfied. We are obliged to keep our wonderment alive and well
until death or Armageddon. As to the matter that perplexes us
yearly at this season, all we may, with impunity, presume is that
an unidentified Magus— up late, insomniac perhaps, bored
with whatever diversion occupied the priestly class in ancient
Persia— chanced to look upward, as anyone is apt to, thinking
nothing of it, and, to his amazement, espied what he took to be
a binary star anchored over Bethlehem again. It takes no lengthy
stretch of the imagination to see the wakeful Magus, aflutter
with renewed expectancy, bustling about his chamber like a man
possessed, donning the regal habiliments kept on hand for what
it seemed was turning out to be an annual occasion. He rousted
his two right-hand wise men from their sleep, and left the young
Magi sprawled beautifully abed to get on with their dreaming.
No point in dragging them along— sluggish, bleary-eyed, and
disputatious. Mindful of what they'd found in dreary Bethlehem
on each of their journeys there before, the three went into
their trunks, replete with opulence, and brought out fabulous,
preposterous gifts no newborn baby, even a royal one, would
ever need. When they climbed aboard their camels, those trusty

creatures headed west. They'd gone that way all the times before, and knew the desert route by heart.

They still do, all these centuries later. In the tag end of November, the days fall off the earth, and night comes early. The hushed season, awaiting the Light, informs remembrance. One senses, rather than hears, crepuscular wings aflutter over clapboard meetinghouses, weathered barns, and sheepfolds. Only an evening bell punctuates the biblical stillness of Advent. The Magi are aware that no one gives a rat's posterior about them anymore. They're old hat. Their tedious journey is no longer "Breaking News" on CNN; no disc jockey interrupts treacly country music on the radio to read a bulletin. For years, merely the sight of them caused a stir across the country, and nowhere more than in Burnt Church, Tennessee, and to the east where the Nantahala Mountains are hoisted in the far southwest corner of North Carolina. There are those among the young who waited for the Magi to pass their ancestral farmsteads, feeling they were as close to heaven there as anyone could get, and still be earthbound. But impatience got the best of them. They moved to Florida and bought themselves a double-wide. The old ones aren't going anywhere. They're watchful at their windows, wondering who'll bring them staples if a wintry mix moves in, curving up northeastward from the Gulf of Mexico. Already, back in October, the Hallmark Gold Crown Stores, not far away in Cullowhee and Asheville, and shops in postage-stamp towns in between, trotted out this year's various card designs of imagined Magi on their camels, in tandem as usual. Meanwhile, the *real* Magi, bone-tired, headachy, hungry— riding camels that are old, infirmed—risk road rage if they veer near the thoroughfares backed up with cars headed for the malls. And so they labor into the heart of the dark, seductive Appalachians.

CHARLES SEMONES   99

Even while their usual devotees wait for them, they lumber into myth.

A handful of true believers in tiny Bethlehem, in Henry County, Kentucky, install a crèche when the first of the Advent candles is lit on the last Sunday of November. But some years Advent doesn't come until December, and that sends the good folks into a tizzy, a blur of frantic activity. They have such a lot to do to get their act together before the trendy thirty-somethings in their SUVs start rolling in from Louisville and Cincinnati and even farther with stacks and stacks of greeting cards to be postmarked by hand. One thing's a given: it would not be Christmas Eve without the Magi arriving magisterially—just as they did the year before, and as far back as anyone can recall. Those learned men, though much beleaguered from such an arduous journey, dismount and kneel at some local farmer's manger. The Christians of Bethlehem never disappoint their visitors, though they be illustrious or lowly. But this year, getting everything in readiness has brought on many a migraine and caused more than just a few to end up fractious. For one thing, casting for the annual pageant turned out to be a disaster. The pimply dropout they picked for Joseph, who sacks at the Piggly-Wiggly, is teenage-horny, having trouble standing still. Gander-like, he shifts from one foot to the other. It's apparent he's badly distracted. He can't be properly attentive when Mary won't stop giving him a knowing look that almost says aloud, *Let's cut out of here in my Z28 and go down yonder in the bottomland along the river to old man Hiram Ketchum's cattle guard and park and see if I can't put an end to whatever's got you bothered up.* Mary, who's the high school beauty queen, is chafing under the yoke of continuing in character, despite her frequent beatific looks at the doll she's passing off as Jesus.

It appears that God—who, from the very beginning, has taken it upon himself to keep the universe well-maintained and running as regular as a railroad watch— may be feeling his age. He nods off, and can't conceal his inattention. Only one other soul is abroad tonight—the swaggering fat man with his ho-ho-ho and those pampered reindeer with their quirky names. Even as I speak, he's hanging tough, nip and tuck, with Hubble through a myriad of constellations. In another hour, he'll visit Appalachia in its sleep. Westward, a tip of the crescent Mississippi Delta could pass for William Alexander Percy's fabled garden in a 1930s wash of moonlight, as if *this* were a summer solstice of seventy years ago. Half a world away, Down Under, it *is* summer, and shepherds in New South Wales and New Zealand gaze at the tranquil sky and wonder if it will explode with angels, obliging them to leave their sheep and head out for the *real* Bethlehem again.

Now, brothers and sisters in the Lord, it was one hundred forty years ago tomorrow that a poet grieved over two sections of this country, so at odds they had shouldered rifles and unsheathed their swords. He could find no comfort in his New England village, and besought the celebrated Magi to pass by him on their annual trek to drab, backwater Bethlehem. Then he chanced to hear the rapturous bells of Christmas pealing hallelujahs from almost every church spire in the land. He rushed into his study and grabbed a pen to jot down words that self-presented. They came rushing like an accordion of winds with a force tornadic. Before he knew that he was onto something good, his poem was completed, every verse of it inspired. He felt certain there had been communication from beyond a doorway he'd never set a foot through. He knew that he had written something that might quiet down the country, fractured, divided, and

quell the temper of the times; he was overcome with a hitherto
unexperienced elation. Though the Magi had not come near
him, he was convinced he'd broken through time's barricades,
and the night of jubilation had spread its arms around him and
would not suffer him to walk upon the stricken, out-of-orbit
earth again. Little did he know that what he'd written would
sound across Christmases uncalendared— and become a carol
which, once the organist at church set the words to music,
the Cambridge choir and congregants could sing each year on
Christmas Day. If folks, unloving and unlovable, accusing one
another in raucous dialects, discordant as out-of-tune pianos,
would stand stock-still and end their strife and, for a day at
least, lift up their voices as *one* mighty voice with the Cambridge
choir, then panicles of love might flower purple—lilacs blooming
in the heart of friend and foe in every late December still to
come.

Each man, we know, must seek the Child of Bethlehem in his
own way, just as those wise men, haggard and obsessive, are
destined, it would seem, to cross and crisscross desert sands
unceasingly, seeking a rough-hewn manger and the babe asleep
in it, the bashful shepherds kneeling, and the angels in a huddle
trumpeting one song, and one song only—not the poet's, but the
one come down from heaven to end humankind's long, childish
peevishness. So I say to you, dear brethren and beloved sisters,
this, as I see it, is the sacred truth, the absolute, triumphant
Word of God I've shared with you on this glorious Christmas
Eve. Amen. *Amen!* And now may all of you who abide in love at
Cowskill River find the long-expected dove of peace among the
snowy boughs of winter. Take heart. God is not dead, nor does
he sleep. There are the harps eternal in the New Jerusalem, and
sacramental milk and honey in an ordinary gourd.

Plain Talk to Hubble,
Reading the Bible Backward

Walking on Hargrin's Ridge at night, he happens to look up
at all *that:* constellations like fox grapes, their luminous vines
threading outer darkness. He thinks of Hubble voyaging toward
creation—a maverick scholar poring over the Bible backward,
through a phalanx of mirrors, to the first verse of Genesis, *In
the beginning God . . .* And in the split second that follows, God
thinks the word *light,* commands what it stands for to be on the
face of the void, and halves it into day and night. And so the
sun and moon. Looking upon them, God likes what he sees,
and calls it good. Creation has thus begun, with its members
presenting in their appointed order like schoolboys lining up
at the watercooler after hard play at recess. But Hubble, relying
only on what's been programmed into it, has no thought of
heresy, and so must go beyond *light,* before *In the beginning
God* to see if there is total nothingness, in which the Being we
know as God does not exist—except in his own imagination.
He keeps a low profile. No explaining is apt to be forthcoming.
Like a cagey, reclusive old poet, he's reluctant to show his hand.
But Hubble, insatiate to know God's nature whole, will stop at
nothing to unmask his face. God, trying to stay even-keeled,
says, *"You will not find me in this backwater absent clocks and
calendars. I'm there where you came from, with the lone farmer
walking at night on Hargrin's Ridge. On your journey home—back
to Revelation—stop by 1 Corinthians 13 if you would know who I
am, and learn the name that I prefer to go by."*

Walking Through the Bible

In the kingdom of kudzu, swamp-light's what we
started out to walk the Bible by. Fox-fire's aura was
a shepherd's lantern God held high so we could see
to pick our way through page by page from Genesis.
But the lexicon was for some of us as puzzling
as hieroglyphics. Exodus and Leviticus impeded us,
reminding us over and over what we could and could not do.
By the time we got to Numbers, those begats got tedious.
They were especially wearying to those of us with empty
wineskins. The desert stretched before us like the floor
of hell. There were those who shucked off loincloths
and left them lying where they fell, like snakeskins
thrumming pizzicatos—not Deuteronomy's nerve net fugue.
Our brief visit to Job's crucible was a downer. Psalms,
Ecclesiastes and the Song of Songs were appled poetry,
sweet to the taste as dipperfuls of water from a newfound
spring. After Malachi, we entered the New Testament
and took the back roads through the four Gospels,
hoping we would find whatever we'd missed earlier.
Paul's epistles sat us down to supper. We'd expected
that. First Corinthians thirteen was, as you might imagine,
the tastiest of the dishes on the table. We dined well,
though not to surfeit, for we'd been taught restraint
was to be observed in all one's appetites. Late in the day,
we met up with James and Peter, who were cordial
but inclined to brevity. Jude, known for being taciturn,
had even less to say. So we set our sights on Revelation,
where the roads forked off with not a single signpost

to point the way. There was a whining bafflement of wind
we found unsettling, and moonrise was an orb of blood.
The old apostle, John, exiled on Patmos, enthralled by the
Apocalypse, left us a cat's cradle full of enigmatic metaphors.

Serpent

Early in Genesis, I strode about the village green like an heir
apparent, my habiliments of a costly fabric, the latest fashion
my haberdasher could procure. I was a lordly fellow, everyone
agreed —my accoutrements appropriate for my excellent attire:
my grandfather's gold-knobbed cane, his antique pocket watch,
floridly engraved with his initials, and the ornate fob I'd long
admired. I flashed his ring, the tiger's-eye he'd cherished, on my
pinkie. It was the look I sought, the image I wanted to project:
that of a dandy much desired by ladies and not lacking adulation
by the ruling class of men. When I first saw her, she was at her
bath on a mist-green evening in the month of May. She had the
look of one whose indolence precluded her complete enjoyment
of the paradise she'd been given. That's when I thought a tart
McIntosh might do the trick. At first she declined, but then
bit into it with abandon. He'd been sleeping, sans fig leaf,
underneath a bower, cloying with its fragrance. He felt the
sunken place, discovered he was missing something vital. He
had a stricken look when he saw her with the apple. He rebuked
her in languages unknown when she invited him to share it. He
said he'd been placed on notice. But she prevailed. The garden
darkened. Then the *Voice* . . .

APOSTLE

It happened unexpectedly, and so quickly. At first, I thought I'd imagined it. One minute, I'm squatting by the Sea of Galilee, mending my nets and humming. The instant after, something as weightless as a butterfly alighting on my shoulder caused me to look up from my work. There was no butterfly. Instead, *he* was standing there. He said not a word, but gazed into my eyes. What that gaze conveyed was unmistakable, left no room for doubt, seemed as if it would brook no questions, no effort to beg off. It said, *I've had my eye on you. You are among the chosen. You'll do nicely. We'll climb the green Judaean hills together. You'll see.* My throat tensed, constricted, and I could not speak. But no words seemed called for. Besides, I thought of something I had read once and could not comprehend. But, oddly, it was as if those words had been leading up to this charged moment. I knew it was a time for silence. Then he walked away and left me to ponder what had happened there at the water's edge. I looked around and saw bafflement on the faces of my companions. Apparently, they were reeling, thinking themselves unsuited to the calling. What had the twelve of us done to deserve it? We were ordinary fishermen and such—except for Luke, the healer. But he'd said, *You'll do nicely. . . You'll see.* Somehow I knew I would.

To One Who Cannot Be a Thirteenth Apostle

It's OK. I was mistaken. You cannot be a twelfth apostle—
leastways not one of mine—though I need one. Nor can you be
a hanger-on and merely tag along when I find someone to fill my
quota of twelve men to spread the gospel far and wide. For one
thing, thirteen's a number I am leery of, and not just because it's
an odd one. And I'm obliged to tell you that, before my mission's
over, things could get dicey—even worse than that. So much
for my hoping things would work out like I had them lined up
in my mind. By now I ought to know that almost nothing ever
goes the way one wants it to. Don't think I blame you for this
latest in a string of disappointments. I'm not out to play the
blame game. There's no room for blame. You've got your—dare
I use the word?—agenda. And I've got mine, which cannot
include you. Turns out, you do not meet my rigid standards.
Previously, you've consorted with certain kinds of *ladies*. (I'm
obliged to observe decorum, and so I use that word advisedly.)
You've stopped by night at certain houses, gone in certain doors
and not been seen leaving until morning. That gives me pause.
But it's no big deal if another hope of mine is dashed like a
melon on a stone. How were you to know that you found favor
in my eyes in the marketplace one day, and I thought it might be
possible we could climb those Judaean hills together? For now,
I'll make do with the eleven men I've got. They're in this with
me for the long haul, so they say. Though I've got a hunch that
some of them would just as soon I'd never happened to pass by
the Sea of Galilee where they were hanging out—mending nets,
swapping tales and such. I suspect they wish I'd gone another

way, though if that's true they keep it well concealed. I caught them off-guard, ill-prepared for what I asked of them. In time, I'll find someone with impeccable credentials to round out the twelve I need. They'll have to do. I cannot accommodate an additional apostle, one held in reserve. But I'd be remiss if I failed to say that I wish *you* could be the twelfth one. You see, I noticed something quite remarkable, unforgettable, and beautiful beyond language that day in the marketplace: *you had a light around you.*

After the Supper

When they'd finished with the bread and wine, they did not
leave the table, but lingered, pondering what he had told them
before he served them what they knew was nothing less than
his broken body and his blood, though they did not understand
how such a thing could be. What words they spoke were sparse,
came haltingly and barely audible. Not one of them took notice
that Judas seemed on edge, sheepish, and eager to be elsewhere.
Nor did they think anything untoward when John, known to be
the one among them that Jesus favored most, lay his head on his
Master's chest. (None of the eleven felt the slightest twinge of
jealousy.) They knew those two loved each other more than what
was customary for men of that time and place. But they did
not get the notion that what they saw was not quite right and
a little quirky. What lay before them was enough for them to
comprehend. How *he* seemed unafraid, self-possessed in the face
of what he knew was coming gave them pause. They were not
sophisticated men. By no stretch could they have guessed that
in centuries to come there'd be learned men who'd devise vile
speculations and crucify the Lord a second time in their minds.
It would be John who'd mock them by spelling God's name *Love*.

Incident in Jerusalem

No matter if their appearance was deceiving,
they were the morning's sons and had no need
to fret about impressions the world sets store by.
It is true, they were a scroungy lot, the twelve
of them, grungy preachers, each one rank with
his own miasma mixed with fish-smell. Their
master set a pace that did not take hygiene
into account. They managed their ablutions on
the sly, but were forced to keep them minimal.
Their mission was to set Jerusalem to rights since
he'd wept when he looked out over it. The rulers
muttered underneath their breath, but it was him,
their leader, who was the one they had it in for.
But he'd gone to Gethsemane to plead with God.
The rulers could afford to be patient, bide their time,
though waiting on some harebrained malcontent was
not their style. Still they thought it best if they held off
until Judas had a chance to consummate the deal
he'd made and deliver the cold-fish kiss. Then they
could weave the thorns, fetch the nails with impunity.

PATMOS

The lone goat foraging
among these jagged outcroppings
does not know the story

the pizzicato wind repeats
when evening comes on shyly
as a monk disrobing,

and the slow burn of sky
subsides when light-years of stars
dazzle over the Aegean,

nor can the handful of islanders,
old men themselves now,
remember how he wound up here—

just that those who brought him
were put out by his claiming to be
the only one of the apostles still alive

and ranting about a man of sorrows
he'd followed up a hill shaped like a skull,
and how spikes driven in that man's hands and feet

tilted earth on its axis, eclipsed the sun
so that the moon came up an orb of blood at noon
as the multitude stood there gazing, terrified.

What the few who live here will not forget
is how, when his exile ended, the old saint
was cradled, whished away by someone sheathed

head to foot in light who walked on water.

The Apostle John on Patmos

Beloved, if I could tell you what mysteries and miracles these
eyes have seen, you'd say that I have been around since long
before Genesis was written—and I sometimes think that God
himself could not be much older than I *feel*. The dampness in
this cave makes my bones ache for days on end; my joints creak
like doors on worn-out hinges. And I must be getting maudlin,
as old men often will, for when I think back on Golgotha, I get
bleary-eyed and can't make out a word of the book I'm trying
hard to finish. I call it Revelation. As you know, I'm the last one
of the twelve who's still alive. Oh, beloved, I remember how it
was, all of us together—him in the lead, of course. I wouldn't
do a minute of it differently in spite of what the Roman guards
have put me through. It's nothing when compared to him falling
facedown, sweating blood in Gethsemane, pleading, *"Let this cup
pass, let it pass."* And God's silence. Then the Judas-kiss delivered
surreptitiously, and the soldiers swarming in with whips and
thorns. Oh, beloved, there are nights when I sit near the water's
edge and gaze at stars—the dazzle of so many over the Aegean. I
think more clearly when I'm close to water. You'd think I'd never
seen the fabled Mediterranean sky at night. Oh, but I have,
I have, more times than I can count. It's the blanket stitched
with threads of light the thirteen of us slept under when we
were thought of as being nothing more than a bunch of rabble-
rousing preachers, bent on utterly destroying the status quo.
The news of our ministry was bound to get to Pilate's ear sooner
or later. And it did. I know now, of course, what all that was
leading up to. Beloved, I cannot forget it—the Thursday supper
in that upstairs room when we knew what had to happen, no

way around it. I saw then that things will nearly always break before they'll bend. Leaning against his chest, I could feel his body tense. He knew the death he'd been born for was only hours away. Don't you think God would have given up his heaven in a heartbeat if he'd held out any hope the crucifixion could be avoided? You think it didn't hurt him to the core? Oh, beloved, let me tell you something. Humankind, clear back to Adam, had got itself in such a fix there was no other remedy in sight. You know the rest. It was a mess. Why even some of *us* got crossways. I remember this: when I saw Judas eyeballing him during supper, like he was taking his measure for a winding-sheet—the whole time thinking of nothing but money—my blood roiled. But knowing that the cup would not pass, Jesus whispered, "Let it be. Just love him."

A Birth at Inverness: 2 February 1934

for Wade Hall

Now it came to pass on no spectacular February second
in the year of nineteen thirty-four that I, self-called into
the ministry of God, self-taught to spread the Word
in Bullock County, Alabama, was obliged to travel by
shank's mare to the neighborhood of Macedonia to labor
mightily (if it came to that, and I had a hunch it would)
with a man who'd let his soul fall into a state of unsightly
disrepair. His sins were legion, scarlet, so that, privately,
upon seeing him, I had my doubts that he stood a chance
of inheriting redemption. Still, as a man of the cloth is
expected to, I gave his situation my best shot. I was on
my knees, washing his feet, and he was making tearful
supplication, when it sounded as if creation had spoken
clear as a clarion way off yonder in the never-ending.
Alarmed, I sprang to my feet, of half a mind to skedaddle
out of there. Then I saw "Fraze" Hall, leaning like time
against the doorjamb. He said, "Miss Sarah Waters Hall
has been delivered of a whopping boy. They want that
you should come. 'Jabo' has what he's been wanting—a
field hand who'll bend his back for free." That was typical
of "Fraze," given to a fierce economy of words. But then
he added, "If we try to stifle him, we'll have all hell to
pay (begging your pardon, Preacher Butler). He's had
more than one nip today and he thinks he's a stud, the
only male alive, leastways in Alabama, who's ever sired
a strapping son—and this 'un *is* a scrapper." Then came

that clarion call again, a multitude of women's voices, those of the living and the dead. This time, there was no delaying. I left the penitent with one foot wet and lit out for Inverness with just one thing on my mind. I'd been sizing up Miss Sarah Waters Hall at Liberty Church on those fourth Sundays when we had meeting, and I'd concluded she was getting heavy with her first child and that she bore a goodly resemblance to another girl her age I'd read a heap about in Luke's Gospel—and *that* girl had a Son known far and wide to be a gracious plenty like a slab of bacon in hard times (and we'd been through hard times). Now I'd been scolded for making that comparison and told it did not seem appropriate. But the notion had taken hold of my nubbin back in the fall and would not budge. When I got to the Hall's, who should I see first but "Bootman"? He was back from the other side again, just for the day I figured (he came and went at will), squatting in Elma Lee's fresh-swept front yard beneath a chinaberry tree that must have been half-grown when the Civil War commenced. Now he and a slew of men, some of them neighbors, some I did not know, most of them I did, were busy pointing fingers and giving "Jabo" the old "what for several weeks from Sunday," as they say, and razzing him about the discharge of his husbandly duties and how, in their opinion, he'd maybe overdone himself with this first child. For there were Jack and Jimmy, Donald and the newest, John, waiting in the wings (or should I say the womb?), to become Conecuh People—tobacco-tanned next-door neighbors to the sun. I said a good "God bless every one of you" to the menfolk in their huddle. Then I went into the house where the women were all in a clutch together, whispering like schoolgirls telling ghost tales. Elma Lee allowed yet another time that she reckoned it must be a heap of pleasuring, making babies. But she minced no words about that being a better reason for young married folks to stay at home, diapering and burping their own, and not be looking to the likes of her to take care of them—she, who'd never married and had forgone the passions flesh is heir to. Beansie spoke up and chided her, "Now, Elma Lee, don't start that stuff. There's not a soul who's in this room but don't know how you feel about the bedroom privacies of men and women. So why go over it again?" Then she took notice that I'd arrived and was waiting just inside the doorway. "Why just look," she said. "Preacher Butler's already here to do whatever's necessary. I declare, where have my manners got off to and hid?" She joined me and we walked over to the bed and gazed down at the sweet young mother—looking mighty peaked. I gave my word I'd cut my visit short. I would not read all the way from Genesis to Revelation. Even an old preacherman knows when a frail little lady's tuckered out and needs her rest. And there in bed beside her was the firstborn Hall, if ever one came forth in Inverness. Stout progeny he was too and as pretty a child as I'd ever set my eyes on. Surely a maiden-light must have shone on his soul aborning. I could tell he'd grow up to be a looker (it's a trait not unheard of amongst the Halls) and he was not destined to be among the common run of folks in that place with a name like music, Inverness—or the whole of Bullock County. I thought to myself right then that we very likely had a scholar in the making, mayhaps the sort that would set down in a book nearly everything he thought. I read a passage from the Psalms and there wasn't any question in my mind but what

that baby took uncommon notice of how the wondrous
English language rose and fell like the mighty waters
we'd been told we'd have to cross—and it might not be
easy—to make it to the sweet hereafter. It was then that I
was given the grace to see how our own Conecuh River,
which flowed right by Inverness, and this newborn baby
might be linked as any two or more can be linked by
blood. Suddenly, as if with second sight (I hesitate to say
I had a vision—though it *may* have been), I could see the
child rowing the Conecuh, taking news of us up north so
that our dull lives would amount to something and we
would not die like unwanted dogs and lie forgotten in the
dust. Oh, Miss Sarah Waters Hall has had no ordinary
son. I was convinced of it and said as much to Beansie
who was fervent in her watchfulness beside me. She said,
real low, "Oh, may our Lord be praised." I'd like to think
I'll be around to see what happens when this young Hall
grows up and reaches his maturity. Something tells me
learning will come easy, but love's apt to get its wolf-teeth
in his heart. No one's said that love can't be fraught with
peril if given too much leeway. But I envy him, for he's
the one who'll go and we'll plod through endless days of
sameness with only changes in the weather and the seasons
to lighten up our boredom some, though not to any
great degree. So looks and love and learning will conspire
like heirloom roses curling and uncurling in imaginary
gardens, going to ruin in the heart if they're not tended,
but allowed some benign neglect as well. I have a verdant
faith that "Jabo" and Miss Sarah's boy will, in time, locate
the meadow, the great one of Kentucky, a place that's lush
with history and literature and legend. And those who
write and tell its stories will be known to him and he to

them. There'll be nights when adagios of the Appalachians
and wind-thrummed hymns of Knobs, resounding
over the flatlands of the Bluegrass and westward to the
Purchase may keen as if they'll break the heart when love
is unrequited. But he'll survive his passions and they will
coalesce in words for folks to nod in wonder over. As
we say down here, he'll shake a good-sized tree or two.
The question will no doubt arise among those of a later
generation, yet to see the light, "When was that fellow
born?" And the Conecuh people, the living and the dead,
will consult their memory and one another, and come up
with the day—the one when the wind was in the south
and the groundhog did not see its shadow and, save for
the borning, nothing happened here at Inverness.

THE BODY APPALACHIAN:
A CONVERSATION IN VERSE

(overheard at a country store near Burning Bush, Kentucky)
for Brandon Joseph Arnold

What's that you say?
I said the boy—
You mean the young man, don't you?

OK. The young man then. Boy or man. Have it your way.
Whichever suits you. He's the Appalachians transfigured into
personhood, remade as flesh and blood.

Oh, is he now? If you'll be good enough to tell me, how can that
be, except in your *imaginings? And, for the sake of accuracy,
do you mean all the Appalachians or just the Cumberlands?*

I'm thinking mainly of the Cumberlands, the mountains in the
Appalachian system that we live in here. You understand, of
course, we're talking figuratively, similes and metaphors—

Two main ingredients of poetry—

Oh, so you know—er, the rudiments?

Yes, grant me that much, won't you? Now this young man you
speak of—is he a poem *you have written, or one you mean to
write?*

Oh, none I've written yet. Just when I think I've come up with a way to translate him into words and shape the Appalachians—I mean the Cumberlands—into lines of poetry, I'm balked. But I *think* Cumberlands or Appalachians when he's across the room from me, or when I see him with his friends.

But you said he is the Appalachian Mountains, not just that he makes you think of them. I'm puzzled by your lack of logic, sir, or what seems to me illogical.

Perhaps so, but we're speaking of another kind of logic, what you find only in a poem or in the earth itself— a logic *of* the earth as well as *in* it: redbud-tapers lit among dark cedars, points of light like specters on the mountains now that spring is here again.

So poems are as natural to the earth as redbuds, are they?

I think so, yes, and dogwoods too, delicate and white as pricey lace draped over greening branches, cascading you might say. And one must mention kudzu. Think of all it covers: junked cars; old barns; abandoned houses, now forgotten, gone to ruin, their chimneys near collapse, their tin roofs rusted through and sagging. And don't forget that under kudzu's where the snakes are apt to hide—rattlers as big around as a grown man's arm above the elbow. A steely-eyed, quirky preacher's dream.

I see. So now we're handling serpents, are we? That's Appalachia too?

Some parts of it. Though I hear it's not as common now. That kind of worship's held in secret generally. Has to be. After all it's frowned on by the law, so I've been told.

*It's something Appalachian when summer days unspool green
legends and the nights are aches we think we cannot bear when
someone—oftentimes a sapling-girl, whose voice is like a mourning
dove's—makes a music on the strings of a Homer Ledford dulcimer
taken from the wall and sung to, like a revenant that's come back for
one more look at earth before leaving it forever.*

You've caught on to what I'm up to. Now you see.

*Well, maybe—but you must forgive me if I say I think you've
taken hold of an idea that will not yield itself to what you have
in mind. Why don't you give it up and see the boy— young man's
what I meant to say—anyway, why not look at him as being
merely human? Why insist that he's the Cumberlands, or a swath of
Appalachia?*

I have no say in this. I have to speak of what I see in my head
when I am with him, when I look at him. He's Appalachian to
the bone and comes as close as I can get to ghosting hounds
and flying foxes on the mountains underneath November's
Beaver Moon, as big around as a cake plate, balanced on the east
horizon.

*But aren't you being far too idealistic? Out of sync with what is
real? You're leaving out the coal mines and the miners with black
lung. You make no mention of strip-mining as if you see nothing
vile about the ravagement that's worse than leaving flesh wounds on
the land. And there's something else I'm mindful of when I think of
Kentucky's Appalachians—call them the Cumberlands or what you
will. I hear the coal trains snaking through the valleys that border
the Kentucky River, their drawn-out wails winding like the ghost-
notes of a hunter's horn that echo in the sleep of those who live along*

*the tracks. And there are coal trucks searching through their gears
for the one they'll need to scale the mountains to the top, and over
them—and then head downward to the towns and cities waiting for
their loads.*

That is true. But I am not the heir of old Walt Whitman,
cataloging everything that has to do with these maligned old
mountains and, for that matter, each muscle in the body and—

You were saying?

I was about to say that there's no dearth of moisture now, and
every blade of grass is pulsing like a body loved . . . You misjudge
my prowess, sir, as well as my intentions.

I misjudge nothing. You—

And there's more, much more to be considered. Let us agree on
that.

*Yes, to me Appalachia's in the country music streaming from a truck
stop jukebox or a bedside radio. And the singers . . . For instance,
there's Keith Whitley, the troubled son of Sandy Hook, now unquiet
in his grave, asking someone he still cares about, "Do You Ever
Think of Me?" Ricky Skaggs is in the mix. And there are many
others. And let's not leave out Mother Maybelle and the Carter
Family. They were Appalachian too. I'd wager more than most are
nowadays. For some it's faddish to claim kinship, however distant,
with Appalachia, all the while flaunting their designer jeans. You see
it all the time on CMT.*

When you bring up the Carter Family, you're going quite a long way back, to the thirties in the century we just got rid of. That's not where I want to be.

But a while ago you were getting lyrical about foxhounds spectral on the mountains and foxes sculpted out of wind and moonlight . . . Reminded me of James Still's first book of poems.

Ah, yes, *Hounds on the Mountain*, a classic now. He put that out the year that I was born. And just think. The young man I've been speaking of is barely twenty, and Appalachian-vigorous. And, what's more, striking as these mountains in all seasons— whether summer-shawled in fabric stitched of sun, or white in winter as a clapboard church in newly fallen snow . . . or twilight-purple like panicles of lilacs in spring evenings, or multicolored as October's Indian corn and moonbow-colored leaves, spiraling to earth as if the hand of God had just let go of them.

I'll hand you this. While I'm not convinced—it's my nature to be doubtful— you've made your case halfway believable. I can almost see a sturdy Appalachian lad I do not know, may never see. What's your connection to him, if I may ask?

Oh, I never told you, did I? Well, let's make it simple and say he's the son I never had, begotten of my spirit—and no less so because I'm flatlands born and raised, and his ancestral roots go deep in Appalachia. There's something mystical about it. I do not understand it well myself. It's somewhat, if you'll indulge me, like Paul's grooming Timothy to spread the gospel in the white-hot blaze of love's redemption. You'd do well to study Scriptures for a parallel—

Perhaps—but it's your talk of making him into the Appalachians that still bewilders me.

I cannot see him as being separate from them. I'll have to ask you to accept on faith what I admit is passing strange—so uncommon that I have no words to tell it plain.

Oh, I'd never say that it's less genuine just because language cannot get its tongue around it. Some things can't be told, you know. I've found our talk instructive. I'll study on it long beyond today. We'll meet again?

Most likely, if you come here often. In any case, I thank you. It's not often that we meet somebody who—

You needn't say it. I'm aware of what you mean. Appalachia is my state of mind as it is yours. Come to think of it, these mountains are more a state of mind than anything—or they are to some. Anyway, I'll remember what was said here.

And you can be sure that I will too. How could either one of us forget? We owe it to the mountains to remember.

We owe it to the people that Appalachian authors write about—as did Harriette Arnow sixty years or more ago. She was among the first to celebrate the Cumberlands and their people. Magisterial writing's what we call it. Remember Gertie Nevels? Nunnelly Ballew?

For sure. And there are writers that are yet unknown, unspoken of. They're apostles of the mountains too, brethren of the word. Appalachian literature is in good hands. I praise the ones who write it.

Our talk is going off in new directions. Wouldn't you agree?

Yes, as such wide-ranging conversations tend to do. It is not
of cabbages and kings we speak, but of these mountains and,
especially, their people. We are, I think, in awe of them.

And who wouldn't be?

Surely no one with a particle of Appalachia in his soul. No one I
know. No one I'd care to know.

And so the Body Appalachian—

—is everyone and everything we've spoken of. And so are we,
even though we were not born here. Appalachia is more than a
chapter in geography, more than an area of study in geology. It is
a windowpane through which we see the world . . . and a door.
It is a roof and mantelpiece and hearth and floor.

It may be all of those. But isn't it just one thing more?

Yes—it's the poem that can't be written, leastways not by me.

*Perhaps that's just it. The Body Appalachian has been written all
these centuries. The great Almighty wrote it at creation, and he
didn't aim to be outdone.*

Still you never know what poet might be on the way here from
the comfy warm beyond Orion where some say Genesis began.

*You mean someone with a brand-new lexicon that no one's ever
heard?*

Could be . . . could be. There's still room for miracles. I'd rule out nothing.

Nor, I suppose—now that we have talked—would I. We'll have to wait and see.

Yes, we'll see what happens. But for now, there's so much earth and human beauty here to keep us busy just beholding—

And don't forget. Beholding is a kind of worship. You said poems are as natural to the earth as redbuds . . . dogwoods too. If that's the case, I'd say that yonder on the mountains are words aplenty, fit for casting into lines of poetry. And the young man you spoke of? Even heaven must take notice. You were hoping that would happen, weren't you?

Yes, I suppose I was. Though, come to think of it, I suspect he's had heaven's full attention all along. The Almighty doesn't mold such beauty and then look the other way.

Well, as I said earlier, this talk has been instructive—not an experience I would hope for every day. Besides, that would make it commonplace—something that's to be avoided.

I am a scryer. I know we will meet again. This is a place past anyone's forgetting—a parchment with two words scrawled on it, both of them in ancient blood.

And what might they be?

Home—

OK, that's one. And the other?

Love . . .

Yes, of course, I see. It would have to be. No other word brings everything full circle such as that one does.

It resonates all through these mountains on as fine an April morning as your eyes were made to see.

And am I to think that birdsong sets the Psalms to music and flutes them high among the branches of almost every tree?

I cannot promise that's the case, though I suspect it is. I suggest you come back and see.

You make it out to be the next thing to the never-ending.

Oh, for all I know it is the never-ending. Perhaps the New Jerusalem. It's not for me to say.

And the young man we spoke of earlier? Is he—?

My notion of the Body Appalachian, yes, for sure. My main one, certainly. There's an old hymn that comes down across the centuries from a plainsong that seems to sum up much I've tried to tell you. It goes—and this is but a portion of it: *Of the Father's love begotten, Ere the worlds began to be, / Let no tongue on earth be silent; Every voice in concert ring, Evermore and evermore.* Those are tones clear as water held in air. They are mist and stone. They're thrummed from the fire of Genesis. What more can I say?

I don't think you need to. You seem to be speaking of elemental and eternal things. Holy things here in Appalachia.

Yes, holy things as I make them out to be—old-fashioned things at risk of being tiresome, sentimental, even corny. Language can get hackneyed, threadbare. But truth does not go out of style. It does not decline into cliché. I will not say more. I bid you good-day.

The same to you, sir. We will talk again. Too much has been said here for us not to. Have we, do you think, become custodians of the Body Appalachian?

Or could it be the other way around?

Ah, an interesting possibility. We must think about it. Mull over it. We'll not want for worthy topics to talk about the next time we see each other here.

THE AGING MENTOR TELLS HIS PROTÉGÉ ABOUT PREVIOUS INCARNATIONS AND HIS DECISION TO GIVE UP EARTH FOR GOOD AND TAKE UP PERMANENT RESIDENCE IN HEAVEN

I

It's not that much different this time, though e-mails like
Mozartean appoggiaturas zip around the world on phone lines
zigging and zagging. If singing speed is not an absolute necessity,
the U.S. Postal Service will suffice. But be advised, they don't
call a card or letter snail mail for no reason. Back in ancient
Athens, what need had we for instantaneous communication
with a larger world when, clearly, Athens was the world, the
only one we needed? I do not hesitate to tell you that times
were much better then, unhurried, virtually devoid of stress,
amenable to those old thinkers, Aristotle, Plato, and impassioned
Socrates, mental heavyweights all three with whom, it pleases
me to say, I and some fetching lads under my tutelage rubbed
shoulders almost daily in that oneiric Mediterranean light, surely
not unlike the holy shine the denizens of heaven revel in. The
undaunted sun's long gaze copper-hued our skin: we flaunted
it as if we each wore raiment stitched of wind such as godlings,
intent on excellence, might have custom-tailored for us on a
good day. We reveled in bodily delights in that permissive city
not forbidden that we'd been told we'd best take full advantage
of lest the sheathed appendage, birthright and birthroot, which
our anatomy boasted—by which uncommon pleasures could be
readily procured— decline and wither and fail us utterly, as had
the shrunken parsnips of old men dozing in the mid-October
sun, sans libido, desiring only the nirvana they'd been promised.

Athens, being heaven's sister city and privy to its secrets, hinted
that, without my knowing where or when, I'd shucked off the
drab, itchy work-clothes of mortality and donned a garment like
the regal ones worn by those who'd made the great transition
and could never get a minute older. I took Athens at its word.
But in the fullness of time, the mirrors in my house, having
no aberrations, and consorting with clock-hands, compliant
with earth's turning, exposed the lie— though I'd been taking
pleasure in my ease, thinking the matter settled. And so I went
throughout the city saying my good-byes to those who had, just
by being there, aroused in me a strong adherence to both philia
and eros. Both gave my nature its much desired completion and
made the garden city of the earth nothing less than paradisiacal.
But to start being homesick for a place before I actually left it all
but smothered me—as a winding-sheet would a claustrophobe. I
packed all my personal effects and, shall we say, *esoterica*— (not
to be confused with *erotica*)—for travel. Soon my name was
called and my time was up in Athens. I went down to the Styx
and, in that Stygian gloom of mist and falling leaves, took my
place on Charon's ferry. When we pushed off, I did not look
back at Athens. Instead, I kept my eyes fixed on something
puzzling in the distance. Suddenly, there was a gust. My lantern
flickered, paled, and things went dark. Being where I shouldn't
have, I lost my footing and fell into the water. Divers searched
for me that night and most of the next day, but to no avail.
And so Charon went ahead without me. I never surfaced. All
manner of variegated fish gathered with impunity and nibbled
on my flesh until my bones were free to take their leave of it, and
of each other. After centuries of being unbodied in a holding
pattern, I chose to reenter earth via some good woman's womb
in Concord.

II

Though I do not remember, being but an infant, I suspect that I
was swaddled, fondled, and given love aplenty. I'm sure I never
wanted for attention from my parents, though I do recall that, as
I grew into a more complete awareness of the persons who were
in the house, I thought them much inclined to gravity. But they
could be jovial too. Nothing about them affected me adversely. I
had become a genial lad. I took great delight in my little brother.
He had come along when I was only two. Being close in age we
played whole days together. I loved him fiercely. Though given to
uneasy silences, he seemed fond of me. After all, I was his older
brother. Later on, I was to learn that he adored me. But by then
it was too late to let him know how much it meant. He turned
out to be a scholar. In time, he would gain fame. Though I was
not opposed to reading books and learning at my leisure, heavy
scholarship that interfered with village pleasures was not my
thing. That's not to say that I remained uneducated. Though I
was not a Harvard man, there were those in town who thought
me highly promising and opined that I'd go far. I became a
teacher. I had no truck with those shilly-shally dawdlers who had
no regard for Mr. Emerson, or Alcott and his brainy daughter
conversing on transcendentalism in their parlors till the hour
grew late. Though, needless to say, I was never of their ilk. I
merely taught the village youth. Mostly, I liked my students
well enough, though I need not tell you they were hardly on
a par with the scholars I remembered from those days when
I'd presided as their master back in Athens. Some girls in my
Concord school became a botheration to the older boys who,
it seemed to me, were always horny and had a faint cucumber-
smell. But I forbore using the rod. I had seen for myself that it
didn't work. Early on, my brother, who served a stint at teaching
too, had abjured the strap. When the chairman of the Concord

School Committee told him that he had to flog, he hurled his belt across the room and stormed out. Corporal punishment was not for him. So he built a hut on Waldo's land at Walden Pond and started living *his* way, memorizing every kind of tree, the shapes of leaves, and how the light involved them. He put all this in his journals. I think he wrote down everything he *thought*. Preferring solitude, he spent most of his time alone. The thing that troubled me was that he showed not much concernment for his soul, whereas I had considerable anxiety over mind. I'd read a sermon the Puritan divine, Jonathan Edwards, had thundered on the plight of sinners in the hands of an angry God who, encompassing the universe, was gruesome and distended in his unseemly wrath. I squelched all thoughts of doing mischief. For credit I was prudently establishing in heaven, I threaded cautiously through a too-brief lifetime in our watchful Massachusetts village. I would not fraternize with a local dandy who seemed to fancy me inappropriately on the green, for I was not of such a bent as he. Besides, notions that had been the norm in Athens did not sit well in Concord. The love of boys, for instance, was thought to be an abomination by slope-faced, edgy deacons, chafing under rough-hewn yokes of self-abuse and put-on piety. Mindful of their scorn, there were those among our townsmen who offed themselves in attics in the dead of night. Self-inflicted gunshot was often rumored as the method chosen. It mattered not that our venerated sage, whose intellect had once held sway and whose pontificating in the village-square had for years been the last word on issues that were thorny, still walked among us in his ruin with his mind on fire—unable to call certain names and place them with familiar faces he saw frequently. Just as I was about to take full possession of my life, a freakish accident took from me the chance to have a usable longevity. You may not believe this, but on New Year's

Day of 1842 I was stropping my razor when it slipped and cut off a tiny piece from the end of the ring finger of my left hand. Such a slight cut it was, just deep enough to draw some blood. I replaced the skin, bandaged it, and paid no more attention to it for several days. Then the pain began, and I saw our family doctor who made no big to-do about the matter. But I barely made it home. By the next night I was seized with spasms. I was fairly sure that lockjaw had set in. A doctor came from Boston, said nothing could be done, and I would die a speedy, painful death. I calmly asked those gathered at my bedside, "The cup that my Father gives me, shall I not drink it?" and bade my family and friends good-bye. My brother nursed me untiringly. They've told me that, at times, I was delirious; at other times, cheerful and composed. Lockjaw is no way to go. But God was merciful and the end came quickly. I died in my brother's arms. His hard love for me could never be doubted or denied. I've been told that he showed all the signs of having my disease and even felt my death-pangs when I'd been in my grave for days. Being so finely tuned, he almost lost his mind. Like the other time I left my life, I found no lamplight in the House of Hades. I spent almost a century isolated, and in total darkness. Bored, and having no one to talk to, I mostly passed the time away by sleeping.

III

When I saw daylight again it was the hottest morning of the year. I was born the only child of parents whose hardscrabble lives were already on the way to being used up on a shirttail farm hardly a stone's throw from the Civil War battlefield outside a village steeped in history they call Perryville. I came in the cusp of Virgo, late in the month of August, which in Athens they had spoken of in lowered voices. I remember that they

spat the word, making known their vast Athenian disgust for
that noxious time of year that robs men of their intellect and
gentleness and turns them into savages. But early in my brand-
new incarnation, everything being newly minted and exciting,
I gave scant thought to the month itself and only dreaded
summer's trailing off into a minor key. Later, I became convinced
the blood-moon was malevolent. August seemed to come with
more frequency than was to be desired and was immensely
wroth. My parents and their country neighbors flocked into the
clapboard meetinghouse for the annual frenzy called *revival*.
That required going to extremes and getting back in God's
good graces after having slipped up here and there—just as a
consequence of living. As a teenage boy, I found the services
both tedious and laughable, though I was not unmindful that
God was staring straight at me, both day and night. I prayerfully
considered giving up the one vice I was guilty of sometimes
twice and even three times daily, but decided that God had
best look elsewhere for a sinner worth his bother. I knew that
what I needed was a wife, but realized there was no girl alive
my mother would consider worthy. Besides, I had taken up
with poetry. Metaphors and similes used prudently and well
was a beatitude I could not have given up for any wife who
breathed, no matter how nubile and desirable she might have
proved to be. And it must be said that Athens still had its hold
on me. Kentucky had dark pockets of small-mindedness, isolated
places where scholars were not welcome—not did I wish to be.
But wondrous things had come along—the World Wide Web,
for instance. Late in my middle age, I became obsessed with
someone who showed up often in a forum on the Internet. His
poems were first-rate, and he exceeded me in getting the acclaim
of others. (I could boast no particular advantage, except that I
was older and more widely published, though, as I would see

in time, very little wiser.) At first, I thought it was in defiance of all reason that such uncommon interest in him should so completely overwhelm me, for I knew nothing but his name and that his work bespoke originality of thought and language I'd rarely seen in one whom I presumed to be as young as he. I was to learn that I was mistaken: he was older than I thought, but by very little. Not enough to make a difference. In time, it became apparent that the reason for my zeal could be traced back to Athens, or to Concord—though I leaned toward Athens as being the more likely of the two. He had no inkling that I went online and waited for him as one who suffers watches for a doctor. Given a complexity of emotions that made me shrug off inhibitions, I wrote a poem in which I tossed out all the rules of grammar, and, either wisely or unwisely, posted it for everyone to see. He had no way of knowing I'd written it for him. There was no dedication, no reference to indicate that it was he, somewhere in the cosmos, who had brought it on. And at first I dared not intimate that he inspired it. (I distrust the word *inspired*, so I say he brought it on.) Not having any clue, he commented on it at some length, and said he liked it. That was all it took to ratchet my obsession up a notch. My mind, too often prone to acquiesce to a far-fetched fancy, insisted on his being another finer Adam in some other Genesis, a hitherto unaccounted for story of creation they had never talked about in Sunday school. This new Adam was clean-limbed, sure-footed, a natural on the Appalachian Trail. Back in Athens, he would have strummed my loins until they wept for joy. For a reason that, to this day, remains as fathomless to me as cyberspace, the Book of Revelation, and why the faint splotch of light low in the sky on certain afternoons is called a sundog, I wanted him to find my poems magisterial— a seamless eloquence of words and meaning—and let me serve him as a mentor. I dared not permit

myself to think that such a thing could happen—though I've
learned that there's a protocol that hearts establish quite apart
from other kinds of protocol, and can be followed. It works
especially well for poets whose perception is generally uncanny
anyway (some even having second sight). Just as I had feared,
our meeting was not *amendable* to heaven. It was self-absorbed,
filling finger lamps with oil and placing them on all the mantels,
gathering and arranging wildflowers for the rooms of new
arrivals, and taking pains to see that they were pleased with their
accommodations.

IV

But, finally, heaven took a moment to consider us, and gave
its blessing. And now, because of that, I feel free to be more
personal, addressing you as *you*, and dispensing with the *he*
and *him*. You know who this poem's to. After the Odyssean
wanderings of your boyhood years, looking after siblings, you
were drawn at last to your maternal grandparents' farm in
eastern Tennessee where the Appalachians start a slow descent
and finally gentle down into the droll, low-pitched landscape
of northern Alabama. I can almost see you, roving those few
acres of ancestral land you bought and intend to make a home
on for yourself, your wife and sons. Near you, almost every
roadside's lined with signs touting the once-in-a-lifetime view
from Lookout Mountain. Others make a case for Burma Shave
and Mail Pouch. There are S-curves in the roads unsure of
themselves, confused in their meandering, and bounded only by
the green delirium of kudzu under which is waiting any scruffy,
wild-eyed holiness preacher's fistful of fractious copperheads in
season, writhing, venomously impatient to test the faith of some
gamey mountain woman who gives herself in wild abandon to
glossolalia and trances. There's no point in naming similarities

between your hoisted foothills and the sharp-tipped knobs
that, like a crescent moon, halfway encircle me. Sad-twanged
country music cranked up loud is what our rednecks, yokels,
and assorted other louts in their souped-up 4 X 4s listen to while
cruising round and round our Burger King and McDonald's,
just like, I would imagine, in your part of Tennessee, where the
French Broad tidies up the syntax in a sentence it's scrawled
across western North Carolina. Back in Athens, though it was
wide-open, the genteel blue-haired set, taking the evening air on
their verandas would have been up in arms. Old gods, especially
those who'd become sedate and sedentary, could not abide loud
noise. The sibilance of breezes counting leaves lulled them almost
senseless, inclined them to remember sighs when midnight was
no time to be abed with sleeping on one's mind. Such a construct
linked them to those tactile exultations that once defined their
lives. They'd never heard the roar and whine of 18-wheelers
lording it over the mid-sized cars and SUVs on the interstate
at night, making a man, picking out a certain Peterbilt going
through its gears, sit up in bed, thinking *lonesome,* and then,
wish I was in that sucker, headed for Montana, and just as quickly,
lie back down, and try to figure out *where the hell's Montana?*

V

You being young and game to travel, know the singing of the
wheels: the one and two o'clock of wheels sizzling northward,
southward, up and down the eastern seaboard. Your first book
of poems derives from journeys taken—those real ones down
to Charleston, Beaufort, and Savannah, and the riskier ones
you hazard into your heart's interior while sitting in your front
porch swing. From there, you see heat lightning blossom into
lilac-panicles—splashes of purple along the south horizon. North
of you, the same heat lightning scissors and stitches the muggy

shroud of dusk into a folk hymn from the *Sacred Harp* or the *Southern Harmony* whose shape notes quiver upward from my Yamaha—a baby grand made in Japan. The incongruity in that amuses me—but not for long. Encroaching age is quarrelsome in this heat; old mortality is curmudgeonly; it gives me backsass. I'm offended by the Judas-kiss which the flesh delivers. It is preposterous that it should think it holds the soul in perpetuity. Soon it will unclench, let go, and be carried to the grave where everything that happens to it in that black, unending pause will be hush-hush, unflattering as flatulence at the table. The soul's a small brown bird, oscine like a wren. Already it is trying out its pinions. Aging got a grip on me, it seems, when I was not expecting it—was not looking. I find it oddly surprising, and not a little obscene, now that the body is heir to the ruin visited upon it: the gaunt face that greets me like a death mask, when it's met head-on in the bathroom mirror every morning; the flabby hips like slabs of beef gone bad (oh, loathsome to me to catch a glimpse of them when I am toweling down); and the cobwebby scrotum, a receptacle serving no purpose; and, most repugnant of all, the man-thing perpetually indifferent and flaccid. But not yet the home-going, not yet the precinct of angels, not yet the lying down in fire. You and I—we are not finished with each other yet. There's still time for you to help me figure out what my life spent scribbling poems has amounted to. Here in the late light of gossamer weather, let me study you up close and foresee the mastery with which you will surpass me at what we do. There are poems to be written that I've never dreamed of. I leave them for you. This time I will not choose to book another passage, climb into another body, and return to earth—not in any century to come. I am tired of coming back, although there is much remaining to be learned, much good to do for others. Perhaps I've loved the earth imperfectly, but centuries ago in Athens I loved some persons well and wisely. And you must have been among them— not the *you* as you are now, but an earlier version of you. Perhaps you were my finest pupil, or merely one of the boys about town whom I met and fancied time and again on any number of that city's streets. You were among those much sought after by the intellectual elite, stuffed shirts everyone. But that was back there in antiquity. No point in speaking of it now. However, let me be at pains to say you did not need to be so wary on the Internet, treating me as suspect when you did not know me except through certain of my poems proclaiming my androgyny, none too subtly. Though I *should* have, I did not hold your lapse in couth against you. I charged it to your youth's account, and put the slight away for such a day when I would have need of it—knowing it would come. Such days always do. Even so, with what pleasure, I felt you like a current traversing the length of me, I felt you *happening* before you happened. Something like anticipation of anticipation, and not imaginary, but substantive: the present you being neither son nor brother, and not, in any sense of the word, a lover—but greeted as if, in an improbable world to come, you might be. What if your arrival, like a bellwether's, signals the return of ancient evenings when I might be the one to say, *"To climb between the sheets with that one is to bed a randy god"*— knowing there are at least a good half-dozen others I could say the same about? Your cross to bear with me is that of poetry. We're nailed upside down on it. So *friend* is the plain, unambiguous word I call you. If I were to say you are my *kindred spirit* it might spook you. But approaching you, and facing roads diverging, I take what Frost called "the one less traveled by" with practiced tread— not quite as a hunter would, but the next thing to it. *Easy now*, my heart says. *Slowly. Do not move fast where love is. Moving fast might scare it away, or kill it.* But I am not inclined to let that statement stand merely because it sounds good. Plain truth must have its say in this matter. There's been enough infatuation to make a buzzard lose its supper. Though we might wish to be more to each other than an aging mentor and his gifted protégé, our association however vaunted, cannot rise to Aristotle's notion of the perfect friendship. This is not a century that honors friendship. Ours serves a purpose (and we know it), but its end is in plain view. *As lasting as a cup of wind,* we may look back and say. Faithful only to words, their meanings and connotations, some poets are not disposed by nature to be faithful to their kind. Their infidelity would seem to be congenital. Targeted in the crosshairs of time and change, you must know that what you feel for me is no less corruptible than what I feel for you in this false, forked-tongue summer of my sixty-seventh year. Now, advancing as if on tiptoe across the door sill of old age, what engages my attention is the God-throb in you, in me, and how quickly our bodies will be emptied of what no surgeon's scalpel can discover, long before the flames begin to gnaw the pleasure bone or, if it is one's choice, before the industrious worms get word of what's transpired and arrive en masse—only to find the banquet room tables bare, save for a few petals wilting, the sated guests gone home, the fire a pale stutter, and the house getting cold.

Coda: From an Early American Folk Hymn

Hark, I hear the harps eternal ringing on the farther shore,
as I near those swollen waters with their deep and solemn roar.
And my soul, though stained with sorrow, fading as the light of
day,
passes swiftly o'er those waters to the city far away.
Souls have crossed before me saintly, to that land of perfect rest;
and I hear them singing faintly in the mansions of the blest.